AF895877

TOAST

TOAST

OVER 70 INSPIRED RECIPES TO TOP YOUR TOAST

RYLAND PETERS & SMALL

Senior Designer Toni Kay
Editor Gillian Haslam
Head of Production
Patricia Harrington
Art Director Leslie Harrington
Editorial Director Julia Charles
Publisher Cindy Richards
Indexer Hilary Bird

Recipe collection compiled
by Julia Charles

First published in 2021 as *On Toast*

This edition published in 2026
by Ryland Peters & Small
20–21 Jockey's Fields,
London WC1R 4BW
www.rylandpeters.com
email: euregulations
@rylandpeters.com

10 9 8 7 6 5 4 3 2 1

Text copyright © Jordan and Jessica Bourke, Mat Follas, Liz Franklin, Tonia George, Dunja Gulin, Tori Haschka, Carol Hilker, Jenny Linford, Hannah Miles, Shelagh Ryan, Laura Santini, Janet Sawyer, Milli Taylor, Leah Vanderveldt, Laura Washburn Hutton and Ryland Peters & Small 2021, 2026

Cover illustrations by
Victoria Sergeeva/Adobe Stock

Design and photography copyright
© Ryland Peters & Small 2021, 2026

The authors' moral rights have been asserted. All rights reserved. No part of this publication may be reproduced, stored in a retrieval system or transmitted in any form or by any means, electronic, mechanical, photocopying or otherwise, without the prior permission of the publisher.

A CIP record for this book is available from the British Library.

US Library of Congress Cataloging-in-Publication Data has been applied for.

ISBN: 978-1-78879-779-5

Printed in China

The authorised representative in the EEA is Authorised Rep Compliance Ltd., Ground Floor, 71 Lower Baggot Street, Dublin, D02 P593, Ireland.
www.arccompliance.com

MIX
Paper | Supporting responsible forestry
FSC® C008047

NOTES

- Both British (Metric) and American (Imperial plus US cups) measurements are included in these recipes for your convenience. However, it is important to work with one set of measurements and not alternate between the two within a recipe.
- All spoon measurements are level unless otherwise specified.
- All eggs are medium (UK) or large (US), unless specified as large, in which case US extra-large should be used. Uncooked or partially cooked eggs should not be served to the very old, frail, young children, pregnant women or those with compromised immune systems.
- Ovens should be preheated to the specified temperatures. We recommend using an oven thermometer. If using a fan-assisted oven, adjust temperatures according to the manufacturer's instructions.
- When a recipe calls for the grated zest of citrus fruit, buy unwaxed fruit and wash well before using. If you can only find treated fruit, scrub well in warm soapy water before using.

CONTENTS

INTRODUCTION

Toast is perhaps the ultimate convenience food, as well as the number-one comfort food. Readily available and always satisfying, whether slathered in peanut butter with your morning coffee, topped with gooey melted cheese for lunch or awash with beans for dinner, it's a go-to staple morning, noon and night. But why limit your toast options? It's time to expand your repertoire, embrace exciting new tastes and textures and discover toasted treats from all around the world.

Whether your taste is for homemade sourdough, a loaf from an artisan bakery, seeded, rye, wholemeal/whole-grain, brioche, spelt, ciabatta, soda bread, baguette or sliced white bread straight from the freezer, here you will find the perfect toast topping. This collection features over 70 recipes to cover all occasions from lazy brunches and healthy lunches, to tasty snacks and comforting evening meals, canapés and even sweet treats for those times when you crave a sugary indulgence.

On the pages that follow, you'll find exciting variations for cheese, eggs or mushrooms on toast – the staple toppings we all fall back on, but with the addition of a few extra ingredients from the fridge or store cupboard these favourites can be raised to a new level. You'll also be tempted by innovative ideas, such as Fried Eggs in a Hole, Spiced Crab on Ciabatta, Avocado and Refried Bean Toastie, Tofu, Mushroom and Asparagus Scramble, Trout Pâté with Melba Toasts, Porcini and Wild Mushroom Crostini or Banana Choc Chip French Toast. Prepare to have your toast horizons expanded!

With more than 70 fast-fix recipes for food on toast, to take you contentedly from breakfast to bedtime, if you have a loaf of bread in your kitchen, here you'll find the perfect topping or filling for it.

MORNING TOAST

MUSHROOMS, BROWN BUTTER & PARMESAN ON SOURDOUGH TOAST

You'll probably already have most of these ingredients to hand, ready to create an impromptu but delicious breakfast.

50 g/3 tablespoons butter
2 tablespoons olive oil
2 garlic cloves
1½ tablespoons sage leaves, half finely chopped, half kept whole
2 tablespoons flat leaf parsley leaves, finely chopped
400 g/14 oz. mixed mushrooms (chestnut, flat, button, etc)
3 tablespoons milk
a handful of Parmesan shavings
2 large slices of sourdough bread
salt and freshly ground black pepper

SERVES 2

Melt 2 tablespoons of the butter in a large frying pan/skillet with the olive oil.

Cut 1 of the garlic cloves into slivers. Add it to the pan along with the chopped sage, half the parsley and a good pinch of salt. Swirl the pan over a medium heat for 2 minutes to infuse the butter/oil.

Meanwhile, slice the mushrooms. Turn the heat up high and add the mushrooms, using tongs to toss them in the infused butter/oil. When the mushrooms have browned and wilted, add the milk. Taste and season with salt and pepper.

Toast the sourdough until lightly charred around the edges. Cut the remaining garlic clove in half and swipe it over the hot toast.

Divide the Parmesan between the slices of toast and scatter the mushrooms and their juices over the top.

Return the empty pan to the heat. Add the remaining butter and sage and heat over a medium heat until the sage is crisp and the butter has turned golden brown. Drizzle the brown butter and crisp sage leaves over the mushrooms and toast. Serve hot.

To double this recipe for a crowd, you will have to use 2 frying pans/skillets – if you crowd the mushrooms, they will stew instead of brown and you don't want that.

POACHED EGGS & SPINACH ON TOASTED FLATBREAD with spiced butter & yogurt

This egg dish is packed with so much flavour that you will be hooked from the first taste. If you can't get hold of Turkish bread, then pitta or sourdough work well.

1 small garlic clove, crushed
200 g/¾ cup Greek yogurt
50 g/3 tablespoons butter
½ teaspoon cumin seeds
½ teaspoon dried chilli/hot red pepper flakes
½ teaspoon sea salt flakes
1 loaf of Turkish flatbread, cut into 4 squares and halved horizontally
1 tablespoon olive oil
400 g/14 oz. spinach
8 large eggs
sea salt and freshly ground black pepper

SERVES 4

Preheat the grill/broiler to high. Get everything ready before you start cooking: mix the garlic and yogurt. Put the butter, cumin, chilli/pepper flakes and salt flakes in a small saucepan. Put the bread on a baking sheet. Fill 2 deep frying pans/skillets with water and bring to the boil over a high heat.

Heat a wok, then add the oil and when hot, add the spinach in batches. Toss around the wok so it cooks evenly and when it is just wilted, take it off the heat, season and cover.

Reduce the heat under the 2 pans to low so the water is barely simmering and break 4 eggs, far apart, into each pan. Leave for 3 minutes. Grill/broil the bread, cut side up, until lightly toasted, then transfer to 4 plates. Spread some garlic yogurt over the bread and heap a mound of spinach on top. Using a slotted spoon, sit a poached egg on top of each square of yogurty bread. Quickly heat the spiced butter over a high heat until bubbling, pour over the eggs and serve.

NEW YORK-STYLE AVOCADO & TOMATOES ON RYE TOAST

This avocado toast was inspired by a dish served at the wonderful Café Gitane in New York's SoHo. Search out the best rye bread you can find to lift this classic to the next level. **See photo on page 9.**

- 2 avocados
- grated zest of 1 lemon, plus freshly squeezed juice of 1/2 lemon
- 1 tablespoon freshly chopped parsley
- extra virgin olive oil
- 7 cherry tomatoes
- 2 slices of rye or wheat-free bread
- a sprinkling of dried chilli/hot red pepper flakes
- sea salt

SERVES 2

Cut the avocados in half, remove the stones/pits and scoop the flesh into a bowl. Mash it up with a fork, leaving some chunks for texture. Season with half the lemon zest and juice, the parsley, some oil and a pinch of salt. Taste and adjust if necessary.

Halve the tomatoes and season with the remaining lemon zest and juice, some oil and a pinch of salt.

Toast the bread, then cut diagonally in half and divide between 2 plates. Drizzle with olive oil and a very small pinch of salt, pile the avocado on top, sprinkle with the chilli/pepper flakes and serve with the tomatoes.

SCRAMBLED EGGS ON SPELT TOAST
with spinach & roasted tomatoes

Slow-roasting tomatoes in the oven gives them a real depth of flavour. Here they are served alongside softly scrambled eggs and spinach for a healthy yet filling breakfast or brunch dish. See photo on page 8.

4 tomatoes, as ripe and red as you can find, halved
coconut palm sugar (available in health stores)
extra virgin olive oil
4 eggs
100 ml/6 tablespoons soy cream/creamer
150 g/5 oz. spinach leaves
4 slices of rye, spelt or wheat-free bread
sea salt and freshly ground black pepper

SERVES 4

Preheat the oven to 160°C fan/180°C/350°F/Gas 4.

Place the tomato halves on a baking sheet and season well with salt, pepper and coconut sugar in equal quantities. Drizzle with just a little olive oil. Bake in the preheated oven for 30 minutes, then lower the temperature to 130°C fan/150°C/300°F/Gas 2 and bake for another 30 minutes until the tomatoes have dried up a little and caramelized on top.

Whisk together the eggs and cream in a bowl and season with a generous pinch of salt and pepper.

Heat a saucepan over a high heat, add the spinach and sprinkle over a few drops of water. Stir until the spinach has completely wilted, then drain off any excess water and season with olive oil.

Put the bread on to toast. While that is happening, over medium heat add the egg mixture to the spinach in the pan. Using a spatula, continuously move the spinach and egg mixture around as they cook. Just before you think it is ready, when it still seems a little too wet, turn off the heat.

Cut the toast diagonally in half and divide between 4 plates. Drizzle with olive oil and a very small pinch of salt, pile the egg and spinach mixture on top and arrange the tomatoes on the side. Finish off with another drizzle of olive oil and a little pepper.

SMASHED AVOCADO ON SOURDOUGH
with seeded spice mix

This spice mix of sesame and poppy seeds adds a great flavour and texture boost to avocado, but also try sprinkling it over salads, quinoa and other grains, hummus and eggs, or add it to savoury breads and muffins.

2 large (or 4 small) slices of sourdough, whole grain or sprouted grain bread
1 avocado, peeled, stoned/pitted and roughly chopped
1 spring onion/scallion, finely sliced

SERVES 2

SEEDED SPICE MIX
1 tablespoon sesame seeds
1 tablespoon poppy seeds
1 tablespoon dried garlic granules
1 tablespoon onion powder or dried onion
2 teaspoons sea salt

MAKES ABOUT 4 TABLESPOONS

To make the seeded spice mix, toast the sesame seeds in a dry frying pan/skillet over a medium-low heat for about 5 minutes until turning golden. Watch them carefully, as they can burn easily. Remove from heat and allow to cool for about 5 minutes, then put all the seeds and flavourings together in a small jar and shake to combine.

Toast the bread to your liking, then top with the avocado, dividing it evenly between each slice. Use a fork to mash the avocado, pressing it into the toast. Sprinkle with the sliced spring onion/ scallion and finally with some of the seeded spice mix.

Any leftover seeeded spice mix will keep for up to 6 months in the jar with a lid.

FRIED EGGS IN A HOLE
with rocket & bacon salad

This is such a simple yet effective idea. Use a cookie cutter or hand carve a shape in the middle of a piece of bread and fry the egg and the bread together. The result is a slightly runny egg with a toasted piece of bread perfectly capable of soaking up the yolk. Serve alongside a rocket/ arugula salad topped with bacon for a perfect balance.

150 g/1 cup streaky/fatty bacon
80 g/4 cups baby rocket/ young arugula leaves, rinsed and dried
about 16 cherry tomatoes, halved
1/2 red onion, very thinly sliced
2 tablespoons grapeseed oil or olive oil
1 tablespoon rice vinegar
4 slices of sourdough bread
4 eggs
salt and freshly ground black pepper

4–5-cm/1 1/2–2-inch round cookie cutter (or other shape, such as heart)

SERVES 4

First, make the salad. Fry the bacon in a frying pan/ skillet until crisp. Remove the bacon with a slotted spoon and set aside on paper towels to cool. Reserve the grease in the pan. Once cool, chop the bacon into pieces.

In a large plastic bowl with a lid, combine the rocket/ arugula, cherry tomatoes, red onion, oil and vinegar. Season with salt and pepper to taste. Cover and shake to mix. Top with the chopped bacon.

Cut a 4–5-cm/1 1/2–2 inch hole from the centre of the bread with the cookie cutter.

For the eggs, heat the frying pan/skillet of bacon grease over a low heat. Lay the bread down in the hot pan. When the side facing down is lightly toasted, about 2 minutes, flip it over and crack the egg into the hole in the middle of the bread.

Season with salt and pepper. Continue to cook until the egg is cooked and mostly firm. Flip again and cook 1 minute more to ensure doneness on both sides. Serve immediately with the salad.

BUTTERY EGGS
with chanterelles

This simple but luxurious combination makes a wonderful breakfast or brunch dish.

100 g/3½ oz. fresh chanterelle mushrooms
4 eggs
1 tablespoon butter, plus extra for the toast
1 tablespoon olive oil
2 slices of rustic white bread
salt and freshly ground black pepper
freshly chopped parsley, to garnish (optional)

SERVES 2

Trim down the stalks of the chanterelle mushrooms and halve any large ones.

Beat the eggs together in a bowl and season with salt and freshly ground black pepper. Heat the butter in small, heavy saucepan. Add the beaten egg and cook over a low heat, stirring often, until scrambled but not over-cooked.

Meanwhile, heat the olive oil in a frying pan/skillet. Add the chanterelles and fry over a high heat for 2–3 minutes, until lightly browned and softened. Season with salt and freshly ground black pepper.

Toast the bread and spread with butter, then top with the scrambled eggs and then the fried chanterelles. Serve at once, garnished with freshly chopped parsley if you wish.

SCRAMBLED EGGS, SMOKED TROUT & SHISO ON TOAST

Scrambled eggs need to be cooked with patience to become creamy. If they are cooked properly, you will not have to resort to adding cream, which just hides an underlying bad scramble. Smoked trout goes exceedingly well with scrambled eggs and the pretty purple leaves of shiso cress decorate it and add a spicy kick.

10 eggs
4 tablespoons whole milk
50 g/3 tablespoons butter
4 slices of white bread
280 g/9 oz. smoked trout, flaked
a handful of shiso cress or radish sprouts
a pinch of Japanese chilli (hot) pepper or chilli powder/ground red chile
sea salt and freshly ground black pepper

SERVES 4

Break the eggs into a mixing bowl and beat together with the milk and some salt and pepper.

Meanwhile, heat half the butter in a heavy-based saucepan over low heat until the bubbling subsides. Pour in the eggs and heat through, stirring occasionally, for 4–5 minutes, until they start to feel like they are in danger of catching on the base of the pan. Reduce the heat to its lowest setting and stir constantly for 3–5 minutes to make sure the eggs are not overheating on the bottom of the pan.

Meanwhile, toast and butter the bread with the remaining butter. Take the eggs off the heat while they still look a little runny, add the trout, give them a final few stirs and divide between the pieces of toast. Scatter the shiso and a little chilli pepper over the top.

FISHERMAN'S WHARF BENEDICT ON SOURDOUGH

This take on the classic eggs benedict is a fitting ode to San Francisco's famed Fisherman's Wharf, a beautiful part of the city where about a dozen seafood shacks exist. It uses sourdough bread, a lemon hollandaise, goat's cheese and avocado (other things California does well!).

4 slices of fresh sourdough bread
450 g/3 cups shredded/picked over good-quality crab meat, at room temperature
8 eggs
120 g/4 oz. chevre goat's cheese, sliced into quarters
2 ripe avocados, halved, stoned/pitted and sliced

LEMON HOLLANDAISE
6 egg yolks
finely grated zest of 1 small lemon
2 tablespoons Dijon mustard
340 g/1½ cups unsalted butter, melted
½ teaspoon salt
⅛ teaspoon freshly ground black pepper
⅛ teaspoon paprika

a double boiler or bain-marie

SERVES 4

Start by making the lemon hollandaise. In a small saucepan or pot set over low heat, bring 5 cm/2 inches of water to a bare simmer. Place a metal bowl over the pot to form a bain-marie.

Add the yolks, lemon zest and mustard to the bowl of the bain-marie and whisk constantly until the mixture is thickened and ribbons form when you pull this whisk away from the bowl (should take about 4–5 minutes). The yolks should double to triple in volume.

Slowly whisk in the melted butter, stirring constantly. Once the butter is fully incorporated, add the salt, pepper and paprika and continue whisking for about 3 minutes, until thick. If the mixture is too thick, add a little hot water as needed. Adjust the seasoning to taste. Remove from the heat and set aside.

Preheat the oven to 210°C fan/230°C/450°F/Gas 8. Cut the sourdough bread in half and arrange on a baking sheet in a single layer. Bake until toasted, about 5 minutes. Put two sourdough halves on each plate and top with crab, dividing evenly.

To poach the eggs, bring 2.5 cm/1 inch of water to the boil in a medium pan. Lower the heat so that small bubbles form on the bottom of the pan and break to the surface only occasionally. Crack the eggs into the water one at a time, holding the shells close to the water's surface and letting the eggs slide out gently. Poach the eggs, in two batches to keep them from crowding, 6 minutes for soft-cooked. Lift the eggs out with a slotted spoon, pat dry with a paper towel, and place one egg on each crab-topped sourdough half.

Top each egg with 2–3 tablespoons of the lemon hollandaise (gently reheated if necessary), and add the goat's cheese and sliced avocado. Serve immediately.

SAUTÉED MUSHROOMS & LEMON HERBED FETA ON SOURDOUGH TOAST

This dish is inspired by the mushroom stall on Broadway market in London where they make amazing fried mushroom sandwiches for queues of hungry customers every Saturday. It's the perfect quick yet impressive dish.

60 g/1/2 cup feta cheese
1/4 teaspoon grated lemon zest
1 tablespoon roughly chopped flat-leaf parsley
2 sprigs of fresh thyme, roughly chopped
2 teaspoons olive oil, plus 1 tablespoon for frying
30 g/2 tablespoons butter
400 g/14 oz. mixed mushrooms (chestnut, flat, button, oyster), thickly sliced
1 garlic clove, crushed
sea salt and freshly ground black pepper
60 g/generous 1 cup spinach
4 slices of sourdough bread

SERVES 2

Begin by making the herbed feta. Crumble the feta into a small mixing bowl. Add the lemon zest, parsley, thyme and 2 teaspoons of olive oil. Mash gently with a fork to combine and set aside.

To sauté the mushrooms, melt the butter and remaining 1 tablespoon of olive oil in a frying pan/skillet set over a high heat. Get the pan really hot without burning the butter before adding the mushrooms and garlic. Toss in the pan for a few minutes to coat the mushrooms, until they start to brown and crisp at the edges. Add a couple of good pinches of salt and pepper and allow the liquid in the mushrooms to evaporate, tossing the pan from time to time.

Add the spinach, stir through and remove the pan from the heat as it just starts to wilt – it will continue to cook from the heat of the mushrooms.

Toast the bread and pile each slice generously with the mushrooms and spinach. Crumble the herbed feta on top and serve.

GRAPE JELLY

This jelly is the perfect partner to peanut butter and toast. Peeling grapes can be tedious, but once you taste the jelly, it's worth the process.

1.35 kg/3 lb. ripe Concord grapes, picked off of their stems
600 g/3 cups sugar

MAKES 1.25 LITRES/5 CUPS

Preheat the oven to 55°C fan/75°C/150°F/ the lowest gas setting.

Peel the skins off the grapes. Set aside the skins – you will be using them later. Put the pulp in a saucepan or pot and place over a medium heat. Cover and cook for 5 minutes, stirring occasionally. When the grapes have broken down to a mush, remove from the heat.

Place a large bowl in the sink and set a sieve/ strainer over it. Pour the grape pulp into the sieve/strainer and, using a wooden spoon, push the pulp through the mesh into the bowl. Discard the seeds. Return the strained pulp to the saucepan.

Put the sugar in a baking pan and place in the low oven to warm.

Add the grape skins to the pulp and bring it to a boil, stirring occasionally. Boil for 2 minutes. The mixture will have turned dark thanks to the colour of the grape skins. Gradually add the warm sugar to the pulp, stirring in 250 ml/ 1 cup at a time. Bring back to a rolling boil and cook, stirring constantly. When it thickens, remove from the heat and let cool and solidify.

LEMON CURD

Hot buttered toast and fresh lemon curd – what's not to love about this combination?

4 egg yolks
100 g/½ cup granulated sugar
finely grated zest of 5–6 lemons, depending on their size
80 ml/⅓ cup freshly squeezed lemon juice (from 3-4 lemons)
a pinch of fine salt
90 g/6 tablespoons unsalted butter, cut into 6 pieces, at room temperature

MAKES 250 ML/1 CUP

Fill a medium saucepan with 2.5–5 cm/ 1–2 inches of water and bring it to a simmer over a high heat. Reduce the heat to low and keep the water at a bare simmer.

Place all ingredients except the butter in a large heatproof bowl. Whisk to combine. Set the bowl over, but not touching, the simmering water and whisk constantly for 7–10 minutes until the yolks thicken and the mixture forms ribbons when the whisk is lifted. (Check to ensure the water does not boil by periodically removing the bowl from the pan. If it boils, reduce the heat so the eggs do not curdle.)

Remove the bowl from the simmering water and whisk in the butter a piece at a time, waiting until each piece is completely melted and incorporated before adding another.

Set a fine-mesh sieve/strainer over a bowl. Strain the curd, pressing on the solids and scraping the curd on the underside of the mesh into the bowl. Discard the solids left in the sieve. Press clingfilm/plastic wrap directly onto the surface of the curd to prevent a skin forming. Refrigerate until set, at least 3 hours.

APPLE & GINGER JAM

One of the best reasons to make your own jam/jelly is that you can make it how you like it. A lot of jam/jelly recipes use equal amounts of sugar and fruit which can be too sweet, so this recipe uses half as much sugar - the jam/jelly is still sweet without obliterating the taste of the fruit, and perfect for your breakfast of toast and jam.

750 g/7$^{1}/_{2}$ cups (about 5 medium) green apples, peeled, cored and diced
grated zest and freshly squeezed juice of 1 lemon
375 g/scant 2 cups caster/granulated sugar
30 g/$^{1}/_{4}$ cup (2 balls) stem ginger, diced, plus 3 tablespoons syrup
1 teaspoon ground ginger
20 g/3 tablespoons peeled and finely grated fresh ginger

sterilized glass jars with airtight lids

MAKES 1 LITRE/4 CUPS

MIXED BERRY JAM
500 g/5 cups mixed fresh berries
250 g/2$^{1}/_{4}$ cups caster/granulated sugar
peeled zest of 1 lemon, cut into wide strips

MAKES 500 ML/2 CUPS

Place the apples, lemon zest and juice in a saucepan or pot set over a gentle heat and warm through until the apples are soft. Add the sugar and stem, ground and fresh gingers. Stir to combine and cook until the sugar has dissolved. It is important to dissolve the sugar before the jam/jelly reaches boiling point, otherwise it may not set.

Increase the heat and bring the jam/jelly to the boil. Let it boil rapidly for 2 minutes, then reduce the heat and simmer for 10 minutes, stirring occasionally, until thick. You should be able to run a spoon along the bottom of the pan and leave a path for a few seconds before the jam/jelly runs into it.

While still warm, spoon the jam/jelly into sterilized glass jars. Carefully tap them on the counter to get rid of any air pockets, wipe clean and tightly screw on the lids. Turn the jars upside down and leave until completely cold. Store unopened in a cool, dark place for up to 12 months. Once opened, store in the fridge and use within 2 weeks.

VARIATION: To make Mixed Berry Jam, place all of the ingredients in a saucepan or pot set over a gentle heat, stir to combine, cook and store as above, removing the lemon peel before spooning the jam/jelly into jars.

COMFORT TOAST

SUPPER MUSHROOMS TWO WAYS

Mushrooms on toast is a classic for good reason. Here are two versions: one rich and creamy, the other fragrant and tangy - both tasty!

LEMON, THYME & FLAT-LEAF PARSLEY

½ tablespoon olive oil
200 g/6½ oz. mushrooms, sliced 1-cm/½-inch thick
2 sprigs of fresh thyme
grated zest and freshly squeezed juice of 1 lemon
1 tablespoon freshly chopped parsley
2 slices of toast, freshly made
cream cheese, for spreading
salt and freshly ground black pepper

SERVES 2

Heat the oil in a frying pan/skillet. Add the mushrooms and the thyme and fry over a gentle heat, stirring frequently, for 3–4 minutes. Discard the thyme.

Add the lemon zest and juice. Season with salt and pepper and stir in the parsley. Spread the toast with cream cheese, top with the mushrooms and serve.

CREAMY MUSHROOMS
with sweet smoked paprika

25 g/2 tablespoons butter
200 g/6½ oz. mushrooms, sliced 1-cm/½-inch thick
1 teaspoon brandy
a pinch of freshly grated nutmeg
½ teaspoon sweet smoked paprika
1 tablespoon double/heavy cream
2 slices of toast, freshly made
freshly chopped chives, to garnish
salt and freshly ground black pepper

SERVES 2

Heat the butter in a frying pan/skillet until frothing. Add the mushrooms and fry over a medium heat for about 2 minutes, until they begin to take on colour.

Add the brandy and cook, stirring, for a few seconds. Season with nutmeg and smoked paprika. Add the cream, mixing thoroughly, and cook over a gentle heat for 1–2 minutes. Season with salt and pepper.

Spoon the mushroom mixture onto the freshly made toast. Garnish with chives and an extra dusting of paprika, if you wish, and serve.

CHEESE ON TOAST with kasoundi

Kasoundi is an Asian mustard sauce or relish, and is also popular as a dipping sauce. It has the pungent paste of fermented mustard seeds and spices. A spoonful spread on top of melted cheese on toast lifts a humble, everyday dish to another level.

3 slices of sourdough bread
150 g/1½ cups grated/shredded Cheddar cheese

SERVES 1

KASOUNDI
5 x 5-cm/2-inch pieces of fresh ginger, peeled and finely chopped
1 bulb garlic, chopped
30 g/¼ cup (about 2) deseeded and chopped green chillies/chiles
250 ml/1 cup malt vinegar
70 ml/¼ cup vegetable oil
45 g/4½ tablespoons black mustard seeds
15 g/2 tablespoons ground turmeric
45 g/5 tablespoons ground cumin
20 g/3 tablespoons chilli/chili powder
1 kg/5 cups firm ripe tomatoes, chopped
30 g/6 teaspoons sea salt
125 g/½ cup soft brown sugar

sterilized glass jars with airtight lids

MAKES 1.5 LITRES/6 CUPS

To make the kasoundi, put the ginger, garlic and chillies/chiles with 25 ml/1½ tablespoons of the vinegar in a food processor and blend to a smooth paste.

Heat the oil in a heavy-bottomed saucepan or pot set over a medium heat. Add the mustard seeds, turmeric, cumin and chilli/chili powder. Stir and cook for about 4 minutes, taking care not to let the mixture stick to the bottom of the pan, blacken or burn.

Pour in the ginger paste and cook for a further 5 minutes. Add the tomatoes, salt, remaining vinegar and the sugar. Reduce the heat and simmer for 1–1½ hours, stirring occasionally to prevent sticking. The kasoundi is ready when it is thick and there is a trace of oil on top.

While still warm, spoon the kasoundi into sterilized glass jars. Carefully tap them on the counter to get rid of any air pockets, wipe clean and tightly screw on the lids. The kasoundi can be stored unopened in a cool, dark place for up to 6 months. Once opened, store in the fridge and use within 2 weeks.

For the cheese on toast, preheat the grill/broiler. Lightly toast the bread, then add the cheese. Return to the grill/broiler until melted and bubbling. Serve with a generous helping of kasoundi on top.

SPICED CRAB ON CIABATTA TOAST

Crab is an incredibly versatile meat and delicious whether served hot on toast or cold in a sandwich. White crabmeat can be very delicate in flavour, so using a mixture of both white and brown crabmeat gives a good balance of taste and texture.

- 1 loaf of ciabatta bread, thinly sliced into 12 slices
- vegetable oil, for drizzling
- table salt, for sprinkling
- 150 g/5 oz. white crabmeat
- 100 g/3½ oz. brown crabmeat
- 50 ml/3½ tablespoons double/heavy cream
- smoked chipotle Tabasco sauce
- 50 g/generous ½ cup grated/shredded mild Cheddar cheese
- 50 g/⅔ cup finely grated Parmesan cheese

MAKES 12 TOASTS

Preheat the oven to 160°C fan/180°C/350°F/Gas 4.

On a non-stick baking sheet, arrange the slices of ciabatta bread. Drizzle the bread with a little vegetable oil and sprinkle with a few pinches of salt. Bake in the preheated oven for 5 minutes, until just crispy.

Remove the baking sheet from the oven and allow the toast to cool. Leave the oven on.

In a mixing bowl, mix the white and brown crabmeat thoroughly with a fork. Add the cream, a good splash of smoked chipotle Tabasco sauce and a pinch of salt. Mix together.

When you are ready to serve, put a heaped teaspoon of the crab mixture onto each slice of toast and spread it evenly. Sprinkle a little of each cheese on top and then bake in the preheated oven for 3–4 minutes, until the cheese has melted and the toast is golden. Serve immediately.

ULTIMATE TUNA MELT TOAST

There are two secret ingredients in this heavenly tuna melt - sliced banana, and a hit of umami deliciousness from a tube of savoury paste. It may sound like an odd combination, but once you've tried it, there's no going back!

- 110 g/$^2/_3$ cup plus 1 tablespoon canned tuna
- 2 tablespoons mayonnaise
- 100 g/1 packed cup plus 1 tablespoon grated/shredded mature/sharp Cheddar cheese
- 2 teaspoons Taste #5 Umami Bomb/Paste Original Recipe (a tube of savoury paste, available in supermarkets and online)
- freshly squeezed juice of $^1/_2$ lemon
- 2 tablespoons coriander/cilantro, finely chopped
- freshly ground black pepper
- 2 thick slices of sourdough bread
- butter
- 1 small red onion, cut in half and finely sliced
- 1 banana, sliced diagonally

SERVES 1

Preheat the grill/broiler to the highest setting.

In a medium bowl, mix together the tuna, mayonnaise, most of the Cheddar cheese (reserving some to sprinkle on top), Umami Bomb/Paste, lemon juice and coriander/cilantro and season with plenty of freshly ground black pepper.

Place a large frying pan/skillet over a medium-high heat. Butter one side of each slice of bread and place the bread, buttered-side down, in the pan/skillet. Top with slices of onion and banana.

Cook until the bottom of the bread is well toasted. Transfer slices of bread, toasted-side down, to a baking sheet and top with the tuna mixture and a sprinkling of extra Cheddar. Put under the preheated grill/broiler for around 5 minutes until the topping is golden and bubbling. Serve immediately.

BBQ HAM HOCK & MAC 'N' CHEESE PAN-FRIED TOASTIE

You can never have too much cheese in a grilled cheese sandwich but how to get it all in is the dilemma. The solution is to sneak it in on the back of something else, like mac 'n' cheese. This recipe is not for the health conscious, but how much harm can just one sandwich do? It's best made with leftover mac 'n' cheese which is not too runny.

4 slices of wholemeal/ whole-wheat sourdough bread
unsalted butter, softened
180 g/6½ oz. cooked shredded ham hock
3–4 tablespoons spicy barbecue sauce, or to taste
2–4 big spoonfuls mac 'n' cheese
1–2 tablespoons sliced pickled jalapeños (optional)
160 g/2 cups grated/shredded cheese, such as Cheddar or Monterey Jack

SERVES 2

Spread softened butter on the bread slices on one side. In a small saucepan, combine the ham and barbecue sauce and cook over a low heat, stirring, until warmed through. Set aside.

This is easiest if assembled in a large, heavy-based non-stick frying pan/skillet. Put one slice of bread in the pan/skillet, butter-side down. Top each bread slice with half of the cheese and half of the ham. It is best to drop the ham in spoonfuls and then spread the blobs out to the edges, gently, without disturbing the cheese beneath too much. Add jalapeños if using. Top this with blobs of mac 'n' cheese and spread gently to cover. Finally, top with a bread slice, butter-side up.

Turn the heat to medium and cook the first side for 5 minutes until deep golden, pressing gently with a spatula. Carefully turn with a large spatula and cook on the other side, for 2–3 minutes more or until deep golden brown all over.

Remove from the pan, transfer to a plate and cut in half. Let cool for a few minutes before serving. Repeat for the remaining sandwich if necessary.

BASIC GRILLED CHEESE SANDWICH

Sometimes all you crave is a basic cheese toastie - it has to be the ultimate comfort food! For a more complex taste, it's a good idea to combine two relatively mild cheeses, such as a mild Cheddar and Monterey Jack. See photo on page 32.

4 large slices of white bread
unsalted butter, softened
300 g/3¼ cups mixed grated/shredded mild cheeses, such as mild Cheddar, Gruyère, Monterey Jack or Gouda

SERVES 2

Butter each of the bread slices on one side and arrange them buttered-side down on a clean work surface or chopping board.

It's best to assemble the sandwiches in a large, non-stick frying pan/skillet before you heat it up. Start by putting two slices of bread in the pan, butter-side down. (If you can only accommodate one slice in your pan, you'll need to cook one sandwich at a time.) Top each slice with half of the grated/shredded cheese, but be careful not to let too much cheese fall into the pan. Top with the final pieces of bread, butter-side up.

Turn the heat to medium and cook for 3–4 minutes on the first side, then carefully turn with a large spatula and cook on the second side for 2–3 minutes until the sandwiches are golden brown all over and the cheese is visibly melted.

Remove from the frying pan/skillet and cut the sandwiches in half. Let cool for a few minutes before serving (and they are great dunked in that other classic comfort food – a lovely steaming bowl of tomato soup!).

BAKED BEANS with maple syrup & paprika

These homemade baked beans are utterly delicious. They are sweet and smoky and so irresistible and perfect piled high on buttered toast. If using dried beans, remember to soak them overnight. See photo on page 33.

- 2 x 400-g/14-oz. cans haricot/soldier, white navy or pinto beans, drained and rinsed, or 400 g/14 oz. dried beans
- 2 tablespoons butter
- 250 g/8 oz. streaky/fatty bacon, chopped, or pancetta
- 2 onions, chopped
- 1 teaspoon smoked paprika
- 2 teaspoons Dijon mustard
- 1 tablespoon tomato purée
- 250 ml/1 cup hot stock
- 6 tablespoons maple syrup
- sea salt and freshly ground black pepper
- hot buttered toast, to serve

SERVES 4

If using dried beans, place in a large bowl. Add enough water to cover by 8 cm/3 inches and let stand overnight. The next day, drain the beans and put them in a saucepan of water. Bring to the boil and simmer for 40 minutes until tender. Drain.

Preheat the oven to 130°C fan/150°C/300°F/Gas 2.

Heat the butter in a large ovenproof casserole dish/Dutch oven and fry the bacon until it has browned. Add the onions, paprika and mustard. Reduce the heat to low, cover with a lid and cook for 5 minutes, stirring occasionally, until it smells irresistible.

Add the cooked or canned beans, tomato purée, stock and some seasoning. Cover with a lid and bake in the preheated oven for 2 hours.

Stir well, then add the maple syrup and taste to check the seasoning. Bake for a further 20 minutes with the lid off until the sauce has thickened. Serve on hot buttered toast.

CHEDDAR TOASTIE
with red onion chutney

Cheddar and chutney is a winning combination but for best results, be sure to use a really gutsy mature/sharp Cheddar here. The chutney needs to have a good balance of sweetness and tartness to make this work perfectly, so do taste and adjust before assembling the sandwiches.

4 slices of white bread
unsalted butter, softened
150 g/1¾ cups grated/shredded mature/sharp Cheddar

RED ONION CHUTNEY
2 red onions, halved and thinly sliced
2 tablespoons vegetable oil
a good pinch of salt
1 tablespoon light brown sugar
2 tablespoons wine vinegar
2 tablespoons balsamic vinegar

SERVES 2

To make the chutney, combine the onions and oil in a small non-stick frying pan/skillet over a medium-high heat and cook, stirring occasionally, until caramelized. Add the remaining ingredients, reduce the heat to a simmer and cook until the mixture is sticky but still somewhat liquid. Taste and adjust the seasoning, adding more sugar for sweetness or vinegar for tartness.

Butter each of the bread slices on one side and set aside.

Without turning the heat on, place two slices of bread in a large, ridged griddle/stovetop pan, butter-side down. If you can only fit one slice in your pan, you'll need to cook one sandwich at a time. Spread generously with some of the chutney and sprinkle each slice with half the grated/shredded cheese in an even layer. Cover each slice with another bread slice, butter-side up.

Turn the heat to medium and cook the first side for 3–4 minutes until it turns a deep golden colour, pressing gently with a spatula. Carefully turn with the spatula and cook on the second side for 2–3 minutes, or until deep golden brown all over. To achieve the lovely criss-cross pattern, turn the sandwiches over again, rotate them 90° to the left or right and cook for a final 2–3 minutes.

Transfer to a plate, cut in half and let cool for a few minutes before serving with extra chutney. Leftover chutney can be kept in the fridge in a sealed container.

LEEK & GRUYÈRE TOASTIE
with Dijon mustard

Leeks are often associated with French cuisine and Gruyère is certainly up there among the finest of the French cheeses. If a grilled cheese sandwich could be French, it would be this one - simple yet elegant.

1 large leek, rinsed and sliced thinly into rounds
1 teaspoon vegetable oil
1 tablespoon unsalted butter
1/2 teaspoon dried thyme
6 tablespoons dry white wine
4 slices of white bread
unsalted butter, softened
wholegrain Dijon mustard
250 g/2 cups grated/shredded Gruyère
salt and freshly ground black pepper

SERVES 2

In a non-stick frying pan/skillet, combine the leek, oil, butter and thyme over a medium-high heat and cook, stirring occasionally, until soft and golden. Season well, add the wine and simmer until the liquid evaporates. Taste and adjust the seasoning. Set aside.

Butter each of the bread slices on one side, then spread two of the slices with mustard on the non-buttered side and set all the slices aside.

Without turning the heat on, place two slices of bread in a large, ridged griddle/stovetop pan, butter-side down. If you can only fit one slice in your pan, you'll need to cook one sandwich at a time. Spoon half of the leeks over each slice and sprinkle over half the grated/shredded cheese in an even layer. Cover with another bread slice each, mustard-side down.

Turn the heat to medium and cook the first side for 3–5 minutes until it turns a deep golden colour, pressing gently with a spatula. Carefully turn with the spatula and cook on the second side for 2–3 minutes, or until deep golden brown all over.

Remove from the ridged griddle/stovetop pan, transfer to a plate and cut the sandwiches in half. Let cool for a few minutes before serving.

VARIATION: Other good French cheeses to try here include Beaufort, Comté and Raclette.

PARIS

AVOCADO & REFRIED BEAN TOASTIE with tomatillo salsa

This sandwich is great any time of day, either as is or with a fried egg on top. For extra heat, use spicy refried beans. Any kind of salsa will go with this but tomatillo salsa, which has a bit more tang, offsets the richness of the cheese perfectly.

150 g/2 cups grated/shredded Monterey Jack or mild Cheddar
200 g/scant cup refried beans
1 ripe avocado, stoned/pitted and sliced
4 slices of white bread
unsalted butter, softened

TOMATILLO SALSA
3 tomatillos or tomatoes, finely chopped
1 small red (bell) pepper, roughly chopped
2 spring onions/scallions, finely chopped
1 green chilli/chile pepper, finely chopped
bunch of coriander/cilantro, finely chopped
a pinch of salt

SERVES 2

Make the salsa by combining all the ingredients and mixing thoroughly, then set aside.

Butter the bread slices on one side and arrange buttered-side down on a clean work surface or chopping board. Spread the beans on the non-buttered side.

This is easiest if assembled in a large, non-stick frying pan/skillet. Put two slices of bread in the pan/skillet, butter-side down. If you can only fit one slice in your pan/skillet, you'll need to cook one sandwich at a time. Arrange half the avocado slices on top of each slice of bread, then sprinkle over half the grated cheese in an even layer. Cover with another bread slice, butter-side up.

Turn the heat to medium and cook the first side for 3–5 minutes until deep golden, pressing gently with a spatula. Carefully turn with a large spatula and cook on the second side, for 2–3 minutes more or until deep golden brown all over.

Remove the sandwiches from the pan, transfer to a plate and cut in half. Let them cool for a few minutes before serving with the salsa.

ITALIAN TRICOLORE TOASTIE

This savoury version of French toast is delicious and filled with the flavours of Italy - mozzarella, basil and sundried tomatoes. Serve with Red Onion Chutney (see page 47), Tomatillo Salsa (see page 51) or a green salad on the side, or even wrap it up for a picnic lunch.

4 thick slices of bread
150–200 g/5½–7 oz. mozzarella, thinly sliced
12 sun-blushed tomatoes
a handful of basil leaves, chopped
2 eggs
60 ml/¼ cup milk
1–2 tablespoons butter, for frying
sea salt and freshly ground black pepper

SERVES 4

Using a sharp knife, cut a pocket in the top of each slice of bread to create a large cavity. Take care not to cut all the way through as it is this cavity which will hold your filling. Stuff each slice with the mozzarella, tomatoes and a little of the basil. Press the opening down to close the pocket.

Whisk together the eggs and milk in a large mixing bowl and season with salt and pepper, then whisk in the remaining basil. Melt the butter in a large frying pan/skillet set over a medium heat until the butter begins to foam. Soak each sandwich in the beaten egg mixture on one side for a few seconds, then turn over and soak the other side. The slices should be fully coated in egg, but not too soggy – it is best to soak one sandwich at a time. Put each sandwich straight in the pan before soaking and cooking the next toastie.

Cook for 2–3 minutes on each side until the egg is cooked and the slices are lightly golden brown and the cheese has melted. Keep the toasties warm while you cook the remaining sandwiches, then serve immediately.

CURRY SPICE FRENCH TOAST
with coconut chutney

The egg mixture used here is flavoured with delicious spices and hints of chilli, garlic and ginger. Served with a coconut chutney, this makes a great brunch or supper dish. Sourdough works well as it has a tangy taste which complements the spices in the dish.

2 teaspoons cumin seeds
a bunch of fresh coriander/cilantro leaves, plus extra to garnish
2.5-cm/1-inch piece of fresh ginger, peeled
1 large garlic clove
1 red chilli/chile, stalk and seeds removed
1 teaspoon garam masala
1 tablespoon melted ghee or butter, plus extra for frying
4 eggs
2 tablespoons milk
a pinch of salt
8 slices of sourdough bread

COCONUT CHUTNEY
320 ml/1¼ cups coconut milk
1 red chilli/chile, stalk and seeds removed
1 tablespoon tamari soy sauce
1 tablespoon Thai fish sauce
1 tablespoon caster/granulated sugar
freshly ground black pepper
2.5-cm/1-inch piece of fresh ginger, peeled and chopped
1 garlic clove

SERVES 4

Begin by making the chutney. Put all the ingredients in a food processor and blend for 15–20 seconds. Scrape down the sides of the food processor and blend again for a few more seconds until the chutney is completely smooth. Chill in the fridge before serving.

In a dry frying pan/skillet set over a medium heat, toast the cumin seeds for a few minutes until they start to pop. Take care that they do not burn. Set aside to cool.

Blend together the coriander/cilantro, ginger, garlic, chilli/chile, garam masala and melted ghee or butter in a food processor until you have a smooth paste. Transfer the paste to a large mixing bowl and whisk together with the eggs, milk, salt and toasted cumin seeds.

Melt a little butter or ghee in a large frying pan/skillet set over a medium heat until the butter begins to foam. Soak each slice of bread in the spiced egg mixture on one side for a few seconds, then turn over and soak the other side. The slices should be fully coated in the egg mixture, but not too soggy – it is best to soak one slice at a time.

Cook for 2–3 minutes on each side until the egg is cooked and the slices are lightly golden brown on both sides. Keep the spicy breads warm until you have cooked all the slices. Put each slice straight in the pan before soaking and cooking the next slice.

Serve immediately with the chutney and garnish with torn fresh coriander/cilantro.

HEALTHY TOAST

CREAMY CASHEW & AVOCADO TOASTS with garlic chives

These sourdough toasts topped with cashew and avocado make a great summer snack. The spread has a creamy texture and such a lovely pastel green colour (and also works well as a dip).

- 70 g/½ cup cashews, plus extra, chopped, to garnish
- 130 g/½ ripe avocado, stoned/pitted and peeled
- 30 g/¼ cup chopped onion
- freshly squeezed juice of ½ a lemon
- 2 tablespoons toasted sesame seeds or 1 tablespoon tahini
- scant ½ teaspoon salt, plus a pinch for soaking the cashews
- 2 slices of sourdough bread
- freshly ground black pepper
- garlic chives, to garnish (optional)

SERVES 2

Place the cashews in a bowl, cover with water, add a pinch of salt and leave to soak for a couple of hours or overnight.

Rinse and drain the cashews well. Place all the ingredients, apart from the bread, in a blender or food processor and blend for 1 minute to obtain a smooth creamy paste.

Toast the sourdough bread and cut each slice in half. Pile the cashew paste on each toast, add a good grinding of black pepper and garnish with extra chopped cashews and garlic chives, if you like. Serve immediately.

NOTE: Any leftover cashew paste should be kept covered and refrigerated (the outer layer of this dip browns, so stir well before serving).

TOFU & BROWN RICE 'HUMMUS'
with red cabbage & pea shoots

It's so easy to blend leftover cooked rice with tofu into a creamy hummus-like dip, and it makes a tasty yet healthy toast topper. Choosing seeded bread for the toast provides a great crunchy contrast.

150 g/⅔ cup shortgrain brown rice, cooked
200 g/1⅓ cups fresh soft tofu
60 g/½ cup finely chopped onion
1 tablespoon white tahini
1 tablespoon umeboshi vinegar or 2 teaspoons umeboshi paste
1 tablespoon nutritional yeast (optional)
½ teaspoon salt, or to taste
2–3 slices of seeded bread

TO SERVE
2 tablespoons olive oil
shredded red cabbage
diced avocado
pea shoots
freshly ground black pepper

SERVES 2 3

Blend the cooked rice, tofu, onion, tahini, umeboshi vinegar or paste, nutritional paste (if using) and about 3 tablespoons of water for 1–2 minutes or until smooth. Depending on how soft your tofu is, you might need to add more water, little by little, to achieve a consistency of thick cream cheese.

Toast the seeded bread, then top with a generous helping of the tofu and brown rice. Add some shredded red cabbage, diced avocado and pea shoots, with a drizzle of olive oil and some freshly ground black pepper.

NOTE: This hummus tastes better if left to rest in the fridge for 24 hours.

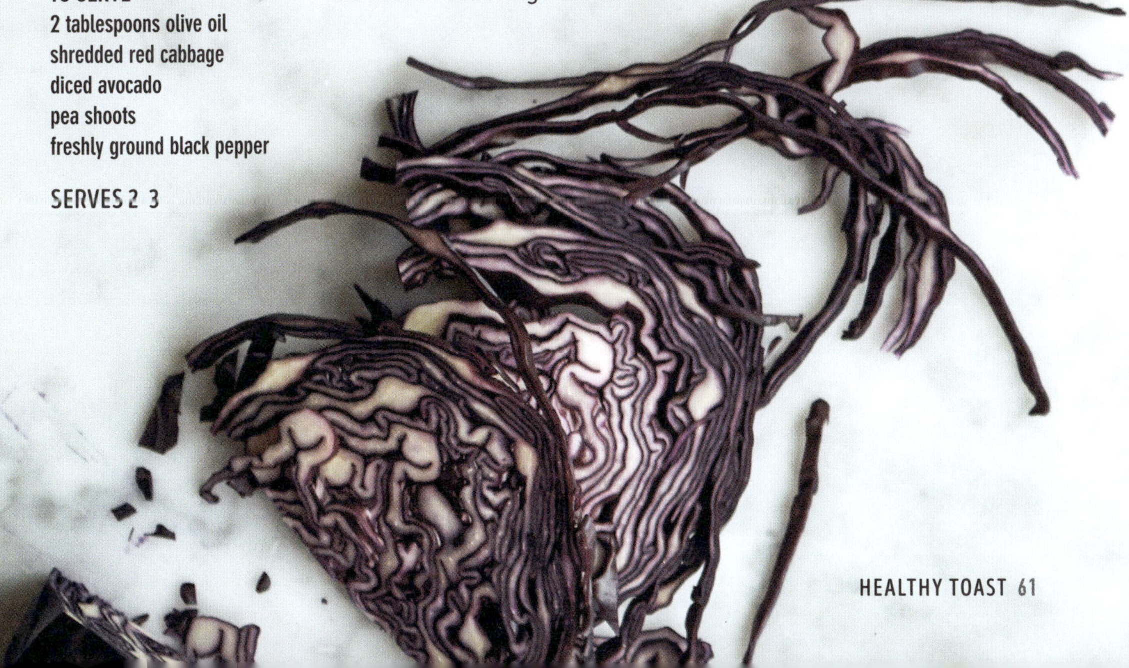

BROAD BEAN HUMMUS

This is a fresh alternative to traditional hummus. The nutty flavour of broad/fava beans works really well with lemon and the sesame of the tahini.

300 g/2¼ cups fresh broad/fava beans
400 g/1½ cups canned chickpeas, drained
50 g/¼ cup tahini
2 roasted garlic cloves (see Note)
grated zest and freshly squeezed juice of 1 lemon
salt and freshly ground black pepper
4 slices of rustic bread

SERVES 4

Put the broad/fava beans in a saucepan of cold, unsalted water and set over a medium heat. Bring to a low simmer and continue to simmer for 5 minutes. Drain, then put in a bowl of cold water and chill in the fridge to halt the cooking. After a few minutes, remove the outer skins and discard, reserving the inner beans to use in the hummus.

Put the beans in a large mixing bowl with the chickpeas, tahini, garlic, lemon zest and juice and ½ teaspoon of salt. Blend to a fine paste using a handheld electric blender. Taste and add extra salt if needed. Sprinkle with black pepper.

Toast the bread, then drizzle with a little olive oil and serve alongside the dip. Any leftover hummus can be covered and stored in the fridge for up to 4 days.

NOTE: To roast garlic, place a whole bulb of garlic on a baking sheet and cook in a preheated oven at 160°C fan/ 180°C/350°F/Gas 4 for 45 minutes. You can easily do this while you're cooking something else and save it in the fridge until you need it. You will now have a bulb of soft garlic paste that can be squeezed one clove at a time.

GARLICKY PEAS & SPINACH
with goat's cheese

The natural sweet flavour of bright green peas contrasts beautifully with the saltiness of goat's cheese and the crunchiness of toasted sourdough. This toast topper really does taste as good as it looks.

olive oil for frying, plus extra for serving
2 garlic cloves, 1 finely chopped and 1 cut in half
125 g/1 cup frozen peas, thawed
large handful of baby spinach
1 teaspoon lemon juice, plus extra to taste
2 large slices (or 4 small) of sourdough bread
50 g/1¾ oz. goat's cheese
salt and freshly ground black pepper

SERVES 2

Heat a thin layer of oil In a medium frying pan/skillet over a medium heat. Add the chopped garlic and stir-fry for 20–30 seconds before adding the peas and spinach. Cook for about 3 minutes, stirring regularly, until everything is warmed through and the spinach has wilted. Season with salt and lemon juice and remove from the heat.

Mash the pan contents lightly with a fork or potato masher, or pulse everything in a food processor or blender. You're looking for a texture that is somewhere between a smooth purée and completely whole, so that the peas can stay atop the toast without rolling off.

Meanwhile, toast the bread, then rub with the cut sides of the halved garlic clove. Spread the pea mixture on the toast. Top with goat's cheese and black pepper.

NOTE: See page 66 for the Roasted Carrot and Hummus toast topping also shown in the photo.

ROASTED CARROT & HUMMUS

Dukkah is an Egyptian spice blend of toasted nuts and seeds. It's the perfect accompaniment to roasted carrots, and brings an extra level of flavour to this hummus toast topper. See photo on page 64.

- 4 carrots
- 2 slices of bread
- 1 garlic clove, cut in half
- 60 g/1/4 cup hummus
- 2–4 teaspoons dukkah
- 2 teaspoons freshly chopped parsley
- olive oil, for drizzling
- salt and freshly ground black pepper

SERVES 2

Preheat the oven to 200°C fan/220°C/425°F/Gas 7.

Peel and roughly chop the carrots and toss with a splash of oil and add a big pinch of salt. Place on a baking sheet and roast in the preheated oven for 25–30 minutes until golden and brown at the edges.

Toast the bread to your liking. Rub the warm bread with the half garlic clove.

Spread the bread with hummus and top with roasted carrots, dukkah and parsley. Drizzle with olive oil, season with salt and pepper and serve immediately.

SMASHED AVOCADO
with courgette ribbons & dukkah

The nutty dukkah adds great texture and saltiness to counter-balance the creaminess of the avocado, while the herb leaves and courgette/zucchini ribbons provide a wonderful freshness to these toasts. **See photo on page 56.**

- 2 ripe avocados
- 1 tablespoon freshly squeezed lemon juice
- 1 small courgette/zucchini (approx. 100 g/3½ oz.)
- 15 g/½ oz. mixed fresh herb leaves, such as mint, coriander/cilantro and flat-leaf parsley
- 2 teaspoons extra virgin olive oil
- 1 teaspoon grated lemon zest
- 2 slices of sourdough bread
- 2 tablespoons dukkah
- sea salt and freshly ground black pepper

SERVES 2

Cut the avocados in half, remove the stones/pits and scoop out the flesh into a bowl. Roughly mash the flesh with a fork, keeping it quite chunky. Add the lemon juice with a generous pinch of sea salt and black pepper. Gently combine.

To make the courgette/zucchini salad, use a mandolin or vegetable peeler to slice the courgette/zucchini into long thin ribbons. Place into a bowl with the herb leaves, olive oil, lemon zest and a pinch of salt and pepper. Toss together.

Toast the slices of sourdough. Spread the smashed avocado generously onto the toast. Heap the courgette/zucchini salad on top and sprinkle with the dukkah. Serve immediately.

TOFU, MUSHROOM & ASPARAGUS SCRAMBLE with turmeric

This yummy way of using tofu is always a hit with people who haven't tried it before, and former egg-lovers are especially keen on it since it looks and tastes very similar to scrambled egg, especially when served on toast. If asparagus isn't in season, try using other vegetables, such as green beans.

150 g/2 cups fresh shiitake mushrooms
4 tablespoons olive oil
120 g/1 cup onions, sliced into thin half-moons
1/2 teaspoon sea salt
80 g/1 cup trimmed asparagus, sliced diagonally at the bottom
2 tablespoons tamari
1/2 teaspoon ground turmeric
300 g/10 oz. fresh tofu, mashed with a fork
4 tablespoons water, if necessary
1 teaspoon dark sesame oil
1/2 teaspoon dried basil or 2 tablespoons chopped fresh basil
2–3 slices of bread
freshly ground black pepper

SERVES 2-3

Cut the mushrooms in half lengthways, then cut into thinner wedges. Add the olive oil, onions and salt to a wok or frying pan/skillet and sauté over a medium heat briefly, stirring energetically to prevent sticking.

Add the mushrooms, asparagus, tamari and turmeric and continue stirring with two wooden spoons. When the mushrooms have soaked up a bit of tamari, turn up the heat, add the tofu and stir for another 1–2 minutes. The scramble should be uniformly yellow in colour. At this point you can add the water to make the scramble juicy, and continue cooking for a couple more minutes. However, whether you need water or not depends on how soft your tofu was to begin with – softer types are moist and don't need any water at the end of cooking.

While the tofu cooks, toast the bread.

Mix the dark sesame oil and basil into the tofu mixture, season with pepper, then pile on to the toast and garnish with a few basil leaves.

BAKED KIDNEY BEAN FALAFEL

These falafel are made from canned red kidney beans and are so quick to put together. You could use chickpeas for a more traditional version if you wish, or if that's all you have in your store cupboard! Served on toasted sourdough, these make a substantial snack or a perfect light lunch.

- 1/2 large onion (about 60 g/2 oz.)
- 2 garlic cloves
- 320 g/2 cups cooked red kidney beans, well drained
- 2 tablespoons toasted ground sesame seeds or ground flaxseeds/linseeds
- 1 tablespoon dark sesame oil (or pumpkin seed oil or olive oil), plus extra to serve
- 1 teaspoon salt
- 2 tablespoons gram/chickpea flour
- 1/4 teaspoon bicarbonate of soda/baking soda
- 6 slices of sourdough bread
- red pesto, to serve
- rocket/arugula, to serve
- pickled vegetables of your choice

baking sheet, lined with parchment paper

MAKES 18 PATTIES

Preheat the oven to 160°C fan/180°C/350°F/Gas 4.

In a food processor fitted with an 'S' blade, finely chop the onion and garlic. Mash the beans with a fork, leaving some chunks, then mix the beans with the chopped vegetables, sesame seeds, sesame oil, salt, gram/chickpea flour and bicarbonate of soda/baking soda. The mix should resemble a thick cookie dough. Use a measuring spoon to scoop 18 flat, free-form patties onto the lined baking sheet.

Bake in the preheated oven for 15–20 minutes, until dry enough to separate from the baking sheet without falling apart.

Toast the bread and top each slice with 3 falafel. Drizzle over a little oil, add a few small dollops of red pesto and finish with some rocket/arugula. Great served with some pickled vegetables alongside.

RICOTTA, MINT, CHILLI & LEMON
with griddled sourdough toasts

A sharing bruschetta platter of sourdough toasts and ricotta, with herbs for freshness and chilli for a little kick - so quick to create and great for an impromptu get-together.

4 slices of sourdough bread
2 tablespoons olive oil
100 g/$^1/_2$ cup ricotta cheese
1 tablespoon dried chilli/hot red pepper flakes
1 lemon
20 mint leaves, torn
flaky salt and freshly ground black pepper

ridged grill/stovetop pan

SERVES 4

Drizzle each slice of bread with the olive oil and griddle it on the ridged grill/stovetop pan until lightly charred.

Put the ricotta in a small serving bowl and top with the dried chilli/hot red pepper flakes and grated zest of half the lemon.

Serve the toasts and ricotta on a platter with the mint leaves, lemon wedges and salt and pepper on the side. Encourage people to make their own bruschettas by loading up the sourdough toasts with ricotta, chilli, mint and lemon juice, and plenty of salt and pepper.

RIDERS

AVOCADO, TOMATO, SPINACH & SMOKED CHICKEN TOASTIE

Bright and light, this is a Californian-inspired mix of ingredients for a sandwich that comes together quickly and easily. Ideal for a weekend lunch or brunch, or even a simple summer supper.

4 slices granary or wholemeal/ whole-wheat bread
unsalted butter
130 g/1½ cups grated/shredded Red Leicester or mild Cheddar
1 large or 2 small tomatoes, thinly sliced
1 tablespoon balsamic vinegar
a handful of baby spinach leaves
175 g/6 oz. smoked chicken, thinly sliced
1 small avocado, stoned/pitted and coarsely mashed with a fork

SERVES 2

Butter each of the bread slices on one side and arrange butter-side down on a clean work surface or chopping board.

This is easiest if assembled in a large heavy-based non-stick frying pan/skillet. Put two slices of bread in the pan, butter-side down. If you can only fit one slice in your pan, cook one sandwich at a time. Sprinkle each of these slices with half the cheese in an even layer, then add half of the tomato slices and finally half of the balsamic vinegar. Arrange a thin layer of spinach leaves on top, then top this with the chicken.

Spread half of the avocado on the other pieces of bread still on your work surface or chopping board and put them on top of the chicken to enclose, butter-side up.

Turn the heat to medium and cook for 3–4 minutes until the first side is deep golden, pressing gently with a spatula. Carefully turn with a spatula and cook on the other side for 2–3 minutes more or until deep golden brown all over.

Remove from the pan and let cool for a few minutes before serving. Repeat for the remaining sandwich if necessary.

PICKLED BEETROOT & GOAT'S CHEESE BRIOCHE TOASTIE

Beetroot/beet and goat's cheese are perfect partners, providing a zingy combination of colours and tastes. In this toastie, the mozzarella provides added ooze and helps to hold the sandwich together.

- 4 slices of brioche bread (or use white bread)
- unsalted butter, softened
- 50 g/1¾ oz. soft goat's cheese
- 2–4 tablespoons chilli/chili jam, plus extra for serving
- 6–8 slices pickled beet(root)
- freshly squeezed juice of ½ lemon
- 1–2 sprigs of fresh dill, leaves chopped
- 125 g/4½ oz. mozzarella, sliced

SERVES 2

Butter each of the slices of bread on one side.

This is easiest if assembled in a large heavy-based non-stick frying pan/skillet. Put two slices of bread in the pan/skillet, butter-side down. If you can only fit one slice in your pan, you'll need to cook one sandwich at a time. Add half of the goat's cheese to each slice. Top with half of the chilli jam, spread evenly to the edges. Arrange half of the beet(root) slices on top, squeeze over some lemon juice and scatter over half of the dill. Top each slice with half of the mozzarella and cover with another bread slice, butter-side up.

Turn the heat to medium and cook the first side for 3–5 minutes until deep golden, pressing gently with a spatula. Carefully turn with a spatula and cook on the second side for 2–3 minutes more or until deep golden brown all over.

Remove from the pan/skillet, transfer to a plate and cut each sandwich in half. Let cool for a few minutes before serving. Repeat for the remaining sandwich if necessary. Serve with additional chilli jam, for dipping.

KIMCHI & CHEDDAR TOASTIE

Melted cheese really benefits from something sour or tangy to act as a foil for the richness. Here, kimchi - a spiced Korean condiment of fermented pickled cabbage - does just that to perfection. The combination may sound strange at first, but trust us - it's fantastic.

4 slices of white bread
unsalted butter, softened
60 g/½ cup kimchi
150 g/1¾ cups grated/ shredded mild cheese, such as Monterey Jack or mild Cheddar

SERVES 2

First remove the crusts from the 4 slices of bread. Butter each of the bread slices on one side and set aside.

Pat the kimchi dry with paper towels to remove excess moisture, then chop.

Without turning the heat on, put two slices of bread in a large, heavy-based non-stick frying pan/skillet, butter-side down. If two slices won't fit, cook them in batches. Top with half the kimchi and sprinkle over half the grated/shredded cheese in an even layer. Cover with another bread slice, butter-side up.

Turn the heat to medium and cook the first side for 3–5 minutes until it turns a deep golden colour, pressing gently with a spatula. Carefully turn with the spatula and cook on the second side for 2–3 minutes, or until deep golden brown all over.

Remove from the pan, transfer to a plate and cut in half. Let cool for a few minutes before serving. Repeat for the remaining sandwich if necessary.

NOTE: Vegetarians should note that kimchi often contains fish as part of the seasoning.

FANCY TOAST

TROUT PÂTÉ with melba toasts

Trout has a delicious but very delicate flavour, which is easily overpowered by other ingredients, so it's important to keep your dish simple with well-balanced flavours. Here a small amount of horseradish gives a hint of heat and a little citrus adds sharpness.

- 4 trout fillets (each about 120 g/4 oz.), deboned and skinned
- freshly squeezed juice of 1 lemon, plus wedges to serve
- 50 ml/3½ tablespoons double/heavy cream
- 1 teaspoon horseradish sauce
- 4 slices of white bread
- salt and ground white pepper
- freshly ground black pepper, to serve (optional)

SERVES 4

To prepare the trout, carefully remove the skin using a small sharp knife and check the flesh for any bones with your fingertips, removing and discarding any you find with fish tweezers.

Place the trout in a large saucepan, add the lemon juice and enough water to just cover them. Set the pan over a gentle heat and bring to a low simmer. Poach for 5 minutes before carefully removing the trout from the poaching liquor using a slotted spoon or fish slice.

Put the poached trout in a food processor and set the liquor aside. Add the double/heavy cream, horseradish sauce, a pinch of salt and white pepper, then blend to the consistency of a smooth paste. Add a little of the poaching liquor if the mixture is too dry and blend again. Press the paste into ramekins, cover and chill in the fridge for at least 1 hour.

To make the melba toasts, toast the slices of bread on both sides under the grill/broiler. Lay the toasted bread flat and carefully slice through the centre, creating two slices of thinner toast. Place back under the grill, with the newly cut side facing uppermost, and toast.

Serve the pâté simply with melba toast and lemon wedges on the side. Season with a little extra black pepper if desired.

RAREBITS with shaved truffle

This take on a Welsh rarebit (or 'rabbit', to use the original name) uses stout or ale to make the sauce because it adds a satisfying depth of flavour to the dish. A sprinkle of summer truffle takes this from being a great rarebit to something exceptional.

50 g/3½ tablespoons butter
50 g/3½ tablespoons plain/all-purpose flour
300 ml/1¼ cups stout or ale beer
2 teaspoons English mustard
200 g/2 cups grated/shredded strong Cheddar cheese
8 slices of brown bread, lightly toasted
1 small summer truffle or black truffle
salt

SERVES 4

Begin by making a roux. Put the butter and flour in a dry saucepan and set over a medium heat until the mixture forms crumbs and is just starting to colour. Slowly, add the beer and whisk to combine into a smooth, thick paste. Add the mustard and cheese and continue to whisk until it has combined and is smooth. Season with a little salt if needed, then take off the heat. You should have a thick cheesy paste.

Preheat the grill/broiler to high.

Arrange the toasted bread on a baking sheet, then spoon the cheese sauce over them. Place under the hot grill/broiler for 3–4 minutes, until they are starting to bubble and just blacken a little. Remove and rest for a few minutes, or you will burn yourself trying to eat molten cheese.

To serve, finely grate the truffle over the rarebits according to taste.

CURED DUCK & DIJON MUSTARD ON GARLIC BRUSCHETTA

As well as duck, these pretty bruschetta can be made with other cured meats - cured venison is delicious and very lean. The cured meats also work well on melba toast (see page 80), or try making mini bite-sized versions to serve as canapés.

4 slices of baguette
1 garlic clove, cut in half
about 2 teaspoons wholegrain mustard (Dijon/French or English/hot mustard also work well)
a handful of rocket/arugula leaves
12 slices of cured duck breast

MAKES 4

Toast the slices of baguette, then rub the warm bread with the cut side of the garlic clove.

Spread some mustard on each slice of bruschetta. Arrange a few leaves of rocket/arugula on the top and layer the slices of cured meat over the top. Serve immediately.

If your bruschetta slice is larger than bite-size, or if you're not eating it with a knife and fork, cut each slice of cured meat into 2 or 3 smaller pieces. This is just because if you pick it up and bite it, you'll probably pull the whole slice of meat off with the first mouthful and the rest of your bruschetta will never be the same!

CHICKEN LIVER PÂTÉ ON TOAST

Pâté is one of those dishes that you'll never buy again once you realize just how easy it is to make. This recipe makes a classic, smooth pâté, flavoured with brandy. You could easily make a coarser 'farmhouse pâté' or try adding other flavours and ingredients. **See photo on page 79.**

vegetable oil, for cooking
750 g/1 lb. 10 oz. chicken livers
50 ml/3½ tablespoons brandy
150 g/10 tablespoons butter
250 ml/1 cup double/heavy cream
tabasco sauce
Worcestershire sauce
1 teaspoon English mustard
1 teaspoon table salt, or to taste
sliced bread, to toast

cook's blowtorch
450-g/1-lb loaf pan or individual ramekin dishes, lined with clingfilm/plastic wrap, leaving enough overlap to also cover the top

SERVES 12

Heat a large, heavy-bottomed frying pan/skillet over a medium heat, until a drop of water sizzles when dropped in it. Add just enough oil to cover the base of the pan, then add the chicken livers. Fry them for a few minutes, until they are starting to brown in places but are not cooked through.

Add the brandy and light the alcohol fumes with a blowtorch (or the stovetop, if you have gas). Once the alcohol has burnt off, add 100 g/7 tablespoons butter. As the butter melts, scrape the bottom of the pan with a wooden spoon to loosen any cooking residue.

Place the cooked livers and all of the juices in a food processor and blitz to a purée. Add the cream and continue to blitz the mixture until it is smooth. Add the seasoning – a couple of good glugs of Tabasco and Worcestershire sauces, the mustard and salt, then taste and adjust to your preference.

Strain the pâté to remove any small lumps by pushing it through a fine sieve/strainer using a flexible spatula. Spoon the pâté into the lined loaf pan or ramekin dishes, pressing it into all the corners and levelling the top. Melt the remaining 50 g/3 tablespoons butter and pour over the top. Seal by folding the clingfilm/ plastic wrap over the top of the pâté. Leave to cool for 20 minutes, then refrigerate for at least 4 hours.

To serve, turn the pâté out of the pan onto a plate, toast plenty of fresh bread and spread with the pâté.

SUMMER SARDINES ON TOAST

These crostini can make a lovely light lunch or you can scale down the recipe to make canapés. Salty, grilled sardines work perfectly with the flavour of fresh tomatoes. See photo on page 78.

- 4 slices of crusty white bread
- 1 garlic clove, cut in half
- 8 whole sardines (each about 100 g/3½ oz.), scaled, gutted and heads and tails discarded
- 2 brown onions, peeled and sliced into rings
- 4 tomatoes, diced into 5-mm/¼-inch pieces
- a small bunch of fresh basil, to serve
- salt and freshly ground black pepper

MAKES 4

Toast the bread slices under a medium grill/broiler until lightly golden.

Rub the garlic cut-side down on each slice of toasted bread. This will give a hint of garlic to the finished crostinis but it won't overpower the other flavours in the dish.

Preheat a frying pan/skillet over a medium heat. Add the sardines to the dry pan to cook for about 10 minutes, turning the fish every minute or so, until they are cooked through and slightly blackened.

Take the pan off the heat and immediately add the onions. After 30 seconds add the tomatoes. There should be enough residual heat in the pan to heat the tomatoes through but not overcook them.

Place 2 sardines on each slice of toasted bread, cover with a few spoonfuls of the tomato and onion mixture. Dress with a few basil leaves and season with salt and pepper before serving.

SALT COD BRANDADE
with toasted baguette slices

A wonderful French Mediterranean dish, this can be a simple lunch on its own, served as an appetizer before a larger meal, or even as part of a banquet of smaller dishes. Brandade can be made without the potatoes for a cleaner flavour but they do add a lovely creaminess to the dish. Note that you need to start this dish 24 hours in advance.

500 g/1 lb. 2 oz. cod fillet, skinned and boned
salt
1 brown onion, peeled and diced
4 garlic cloves, peeled and thinly sliced
200 g/7 oz. Maris Piper/Russet potatoes, peeled and diced
200 ml/3/4 cup whole milk
100 ml/1/3 cup olive oil, plus extra for drizzling
100 ml/1/3 cup double/heavy cream
1 baguette, sliced diagonally into 5-mm/1/4-inch slices

TO SERVE
1 cucumber, peeled and finely diced
a small bunch of fresh dill, finely chopped
1 small fennel bulb, thinly sliced
grated zest and freshly squeezed juice of 1 lemon

SERVES 8–10

Generously season the cod fillet with salt on both sides and set in the fridge for at least 24 hours.

Begin by making the salad. Toss the cucumber, dill, fennel and lemon zest and juice together in a large mixing bowl. Set aside for at least 1 hour in advance so the flavours can combine and to mute the fennel slightly.

Rinse the cod fillet and pat dry, then put the cod, onion, garlic, potatoes and milk in a saucepan set over a gentle heat. Bring to a low simmer for 20 minutes, check the potatoes are fully cooked, then strain off any excess milk.

While still hot, transfer the mixture to a food processor and blend. With the motor running, slowly pour in the oil and double/heavy cream. You should now have a thick paste. Transfer to a serving bowl.

Toast the bread slices under a medium grill/broiler until lightly golden.

Serve the brandade, drizzled with oil and sprinkled with black pepper, alongside the salad and toasts.

STEAK TARTARE
with mustard cheese toasts

This combination of ingredients is exquisite. The mustardy-cheesey toasts perfectly complement the steak tartare - a very fine supper dish for a special occasion.

2 tablespoons Dijon mustard
4 anchovy fillets, finely diced
2 tablespoons tomato ketchup
1 tablespoon Worcestershire sauce
Tabasco sauce, to taste
1 small onion, finely chopped
2 tablespoons capers, finely chopped
2 tablespoons finely chopped cornichons
2 tablespoons finely chopped flat-leaf parsley
500 g/1 lb. 2 oz. beef sirloin, diced very finely (don't use a food processor)
4 quail egg yolks (or 2 ordinary egg yolks)
salt and freshly ground black pepper
rocket/arugula, to serve

MUSTARD CHEESE TOASTS
2 tablespoons butter, melted
1 tablespoon hot English mustard
75 g/3/4 cup grated/shredded Cheddar cheese
1 baguette, sliced into 1-cm/1/2-inch slices

SERVES 4

Put the Dijon mustard, anchovies, ketchup and Worcestershire sauce in a large bowl and whisk. Add the onion, capers, cornichons and parsley.

Add the chopped beef to the bowl and mix well using a spoon. Season with salt and pepper and Tabasco, to taste. Divide the meat evenly among 4 chilled dinner plates.

Wash the quail egg shells well. Separate the quail eggs and nestle the yolks in half-shells on top of the tartare, for guests to mix as they like. (If you don't have quail eggs, use 2 egg yolks and whisk them with the mustard and ketchup mixture.)

To make the mustard cheese toasts, combine the melted butter and English mustard and brush the mixture over the slices of baguette. Top with cheese and grill/broil for 5 minutes, until the tops are melted and bubbly. Serve with the steak tartare and rocket/arugula on the side.

SERRANO HAM & AUBERGINE ON TOASTED SODA BREAD

An open sandwich on toasted soda bread is just the thing if you have the taste for something a bit fancier than a plain sandwich. Go for a mixture of textures and flavours - here you have crunchy toast paired with soft ham, plus mild aubergine/eggplant contrasting with a lightly spiced salsa.

8 thin (5-mm/¼-inch thick) slices aubergine/eggplant
olive oil, for brushing
4 slices of fresh soda bread or crusty wholemeal/ whole-wheat bread
Tomatillo Salsa (see page 51), for spreading, or use a relish of your choice
8 slices of Serrano ham (or use coppa or prosciutto, if you prefer)
finely chopped fresh flat-leaf parsley, to garnish
Parmesan shavings, to serve
sea salt and freshly ground black pepper

MAKES 4

Preheat the grill/broiler to high.

Put the aubergine/eggplant slices in a single layer on a baking sheet. Brush olive oil on both sides of the slices so that they're well covered, then sprinkle with salt and pepper on both sides. Grill/broil under the preheated grill/broiler for 5 minutes on each side, turning once. Remove from the heat.

Meanwhile, lightly toast the soda bread.

For each open sandwich, put a good spread of the salsa on a slice of toast. Put 2 grilled/ broiled aubergine/eggplant slices on top and then ruffle 2 slices of the Serrano ham along the top. (You can shred the ham first, if you prefer, or serve it with a knife and fork so that the ham doesn't tear off the top with the first bite.) Garnish with freshly chopped parsley and Parmesan shavings and add a little salt and pepper. Serve immediately.

LOBSTER & BEAUFORT BRIOCHE TOASTIE with tarragon mayo

This recipe lifts toasties to a new level of excellence! It combines lobster with Beaufort cheese (a firm, fruity French cheese) and brioche, with tarragon mayonnaise providing the perfect finishing touch.

2–3 tablespoons mayonnaise
a small handful of fresh tarragon leaves, chopped
1 teaspoon freshly squeezed lemon juice
4 large slices of brioche bread
about 250 g/9 oz. lobster meat, cooked
250 g/3 cups grated/shredded Beaufort cheese
unsalted butter, softened
freshly ground black pepper

SERVES 2

In a small bowl, combine the mayonnaise, tarragon, lemon juice and a generous pinch of black pepper. Stir well and set aside.

Butter the brioche slices on one side and arrange buttered-side down on a clean work surface or chopping board. Spread two of the non-buttered sides generously with the tarragon mayonnaise.

Assemble just before cooking, in a large, heavy-based non-stick frying pan/skillet. Depending on the size of your pan/skillet, you may need to cook one sandwich at a time; if the pan is large enough, place two of the bread slices not spread with tarragon mayonnaise in the pan, buttered-side down. Top each of these slices with half of the cheese, taking care not to let too much fall into the pan. Top this with half the lobster, arranging in an even layer over all. Finally, enclose with the mayonnaise-coated slices of brioche, buttered-side up.

Turn the heat to medium and cook the first side for 3–4 minutes until deep golden, pressing gently with a large spatula. Carefully turn with the spatula and cook on the other side, for 2–3 minutes more or until deep golden brown all over.

Remove from the pan/skillet and let cool for a few minutes before serving. Repeat for the remaining sandwich if necessary.

HOT STEAK SANDWICH with beetroot jam & blue cheese dressing

Beetroot/beet and blue cheese is a classic combination, and one that works really well with beef, which is strong enough to hold its own with these gutsy flavours.

4 x 150-g/$5^1/_2$-oz. rump steaks
olive oil
8 slices of sourdough bread
80 g/$1^2/_3$ cups watercress
2 large tomatoes, sliced

BEETROOT/BEET JAM/JELLY
500 g/$3^1/_4$ cups roughly chopped beetroots/beets
50 g/4 tablespoons finely grated fresh horseradish
100 ml/$^1/_3$ cup balsamic vinegar
50 g/$^1/_4$ cup light brown sugar
1 teaspoon sea salt

BLUE CHEESE DRESSING
60 g/$^1/_4$ cup sour/soured cream
60 ml/$^1/_4$ cup buttermilk
1 tablespoon freshly squeezed lemon juice
1 tablespoon freshly chopped dill
$^1/_2$ teaspoon sea salt
100 g/$^3/_4$ cup crumbled Stilton or other blue cheese
freshly ground black pepper

SERVES 4

Begin by preparing the beetroot/beet jam/jelly. Put the beetroots/beets in a saucepan or pot of boiling water and cook for about 40 minutes, until just tender. Drain and set aside to cool.

Once cool enough to handle, peel and grate into a clean, large saucepan or pot. Add all the other ingredients, set the pan over a gentle heat and simmer for 30–40 minutes until there is no liquid and the beetroots/ beets are of a jammy consistency. Remove from the heat and set aside.

To make the blue cheese dressing, put the sour/soured cream, buttermilk, lemon juice, dill, salt and pepper in a mixing bowl and mix well. Add the crumbled Stilton, stir through and set aside.

Rub the steaks with olive oil and season with salt and pepper.

Place a ridged griddle/grill pan over a high heat and get it really hot before placing the steaks into it. Cook for about 3 minutes on each side, then place on a plate and cover with foil to allow the meat to rest.

Lightly toast the sourdough bread and spread a generous layer of beetroot/beet jam/jelly on the bottom of four of the slices. Add a layer of watercress and top with sliced tomato.

Slice the rested steaks on the diagonal into 1-cm/$^1/_2$-inch slices and arrange over the tomato. Spoon some blue cheese dressing on top of the warm steak so that the cheese starts to melt and place the other slices of toasted bread on top. Serve immediately.

CHORIZO, MINI PEPPERS & MANCHEGO TOASTIE

This decidedly Spanish-inspired treat features a magical combination of spicy, smoky chorizo, sweet mini peppers and creamy Manchego. If you want a little extra ooziness, replace some of the Manchego with mozzarella. If you're a spice fan, why not substitute the sweet peppers for padrón peppers for an extra kick.

1–2 tablespoons extra virgin olive oil
100 g/3½ oz. mini (bell) peppers or padrón peppers
salt
unsalted butter, softened
4 slices of sourdough bread
100 g/3½ oz. chorizo, thinly sliced
250 g/3 cups grated/shredded Manchego cheese

SERVES 2

Heat the oil in a small frying pan/skillet and add the peppers. Cook over a medium heat for 5–10 minutes until charred all over. Season lightly with salt and set aside.

Butter the bread slices on one side and arrange buttered-side down on a clean work surface or chopping board.

Divide the chorizo in half and arrange on two slices of bread. Next, divide the cheese in half and sprinkle two-thirds of each on top. Top with 3 or 4 peppers, then the remaining cheese. Enclose with the remaining bread, buttered-side up.

Place the two sandwiches in a large, heavy-based non-stick frying pan/skillet. Depending on the size of your pan/skillet, you may need to cook one sandwich at a time.

Turn the heat to medium and cook for 3–4 minutes on the first side. Carefully turn with a large spatula and cook on the second side, for 2–3 minutes more, pressing down gently on this side until golden brown all over.

Remove from the pan/skillet and let cool for a few minutes before serving.

BRIE & APPLE-CRANBERRY SAUCE WALNUT BREAD TOASTIE

Most nuts go brilliantly with Brie and cranberries, so if walnut bread is not available, feel free to substitute something else. Thin slices of Brie melt more easily so keep the cheese well chilled, which makes it easier to slice.

about 180g/6 oz. ripe chilled Brie, rind removed, sliced thinly or finely diced
4–8 slices walnut bread, depending on size of loaf
unsalted butter, softened

APPLE-CRANBERRY SAUCE
300 g/3 cups cranberries, fresh or frozen
freshly squeezed juice of 1 orange
1 small tart cooking apple, such as Cox, peeled and diced
about 3 tablespoons caster/granulated sugar, or more to taste

SERVES 2

For the apple-cranberry sauce, combine all the ingredients in a saucepan over a low heat. Stir the mixture often, until the sugar dissolves and the cranberries begin to pop and disintegrate. If the mixture is too dry, add a small amount of water. Cover and simmer gently until the cranberries are tender and the mixture has a jam-like consistency; keep checking to see if the mixture is drying out – if it is, add more water bit-by-bit to prevent the mixture from thickening and burning. Taste and adjust sweetness to your liking. Set aside until needed.

Butter the bread slices on one side and set aside.

This is easiest if assembled in the pan. Without turning the heat on, place two slices of bread in a large, heavy-based non-stick frying pan/skillet, butter-side down. If you can't fit two slices side-by-side in the pan/skillet, you'll need to cook them in two batches. Spread the slices generously with cranberry sauce, then top with Brie slices. Cover with the remaining bread slices, butter-side up.

Turn the heat to medium and cook the first side for 3–5 minutes until it turns a deep golden colour, pressing gently with a spatula. Carefully turn with the spatula and cook on the second side for 2–3 minutes, or until deep golden brown all over.

Remove from the frying pan/skillet and transfer to a plate. Let cool for a few minutes before serving along with extra apple-cranberry sauce on the side. (Any leftover sauce can be kept in the fridge in a sealed container.)

CHICORY, BLUE CHEESE, SERRANO & WALNUT PESTO PAN-FRIED TOASTIE

Salty, bitter, sweet and nutty flavours all collide in this decadent and delicious Iberian-inspired sandwich. Perfect served with a glass of chilled Spanish white for an out-of-the-ordinary midweek supper.

- 1 large chicory/endive, halved and thinly sliced lengthwise
- 1 tablespoon butter
- 1 tablespoon vegetable oil
- 125 ml/$^1/_2$ cup dry white wine
- 4 slices of white bread
- unsalted butter, softened
- 90 g/3 oz. soft blue cheese, at room temperature
- 2 thin slices of Gouda or Fontina cheese
- 4–6 slices of Serrano ham

WALNUT PESTO

- 100g/1 cup walnut pieces
- 80 g/1 cup grated/shredded Parmesan cheese
- a small bunch of fresh flat-leaf parsley, leaves stripped
- 1 garlic clove, peeled
- about 150 ml/$^2/_3$ cup rapeseed/canola oil
- a drizzle of honey
- salt and freshly ground black pepper
- freshly squeezed juice of $^1/_2$ lemon, or more to taste

SERVES 2

For the walnut pesto, combine all the ingredients in a food processor and process until it forms a spreadable paste. Taste and add more salt, pepper and lemon juice as required. Set aside.

Combine the chicory/endive slivers, butter and oil in a non-stick frying pan/skillet and cook over a medium heat until soft and starting to brown. Add the wine, boil for 1 minute, then season, lower the heat, cover and simmer for 5 minutes. Remove the lid and continue cooking gently until the liquid evaporates. Then coarsely chop the chicory/endive and set aside.

Spread softened butter on each of the bread slices on one side. Spread two of the slices with the blue cheese, evenly divided, on the other side and spread the remaining two slices with pesto on the non-buttered side.

This is easiest if assembled in a large, heavy-based non-stick frying pan/skillet. Put the pesto-covered slices of bread in the pan/skillet, butter-side down. Top each with one slice of cheese, half of the chicory/endive and half of the ham. Finally, top with the blue cheese bread slices, butter side up.

Turn the heat to medium and cook the first side for 3–5 minutes until deep golden, pressing gently with a spatula. Carefully turn with a large spatula and cook on the other side, for 2–3 minutes more or until deep golden brown all over.

Remove from the pan/skillet and transfer to a plate. Let cool for a few minutes before serving. Repeat for the remaining sandwich if necessary.

TINY TOAST

FETTUNTA

The original 'garlic bread', this Italian dish is traditionally made using the new season's olive oil, although any good-quality extra virgin olive oil can be used. In classic Italian fashion, simple ingredients combine to great effect. The name translates literally as 'oily slice', but it is far more delicious than this name may suggest. Although quick and simple to make, it is incredibly tasty. Try it!

4 thick slices of rustic bread
1 garlic clove, cut in half
4 tablespoons extra virgin olive oil
salt (optional)

MAKES 4 SLICES

Preheat a griddle/ridged stovetop pan until hot. Griddle the bread for 2–3 minutes on each side until golden-brown and nicely striped. If you don't have a griddle pan, preheat a grill/broiler and toast until golden brown on each side.

Immediately rub one side of each slice with the cut side of the garlic clove. Pour a tablespoon of olive oil over each slice. Add a pinch of salt, if using, and serve at once.

PAN CATALAN

Simple pleasures are often the best. This classic Spanish snack goes perfectly with traditional Spanish serrano ham.

10 slices of rustic bread
1 garlic clove, cut in half
2 ripe, juicy tomatoes, halved
extra virgin olive oil, to taste
a pinch of salt

MAKES 20

Begin by toasting the bread slices under a grill/broiler until lightly golden on one side only.

Rub the cut side of the garlic over the toasted side of each bread slice. Rub the tomatoes cut-side down over the bread in the same way.

Cut each slice in half, drizzle generously with oil and season with a touch of salt. Serve at once.

WALNUT & RED PEPPER PÂTÉ
on mini toasts

This hummus-style pâté is perfect for serving on mini toasts as a canapé. It can be made well in advance - it will taste even better if it sits in the fridge for a couple of days, making it an ideal choice when you want to get ahead cooking for a party.

- 300 g/2 cups walnuts, shelled
- 80 g/⅔ cup diced onion
- ½ bunch of fresh flat-leaf parsley
- 2 tablespoons olive oil
- 1 tablespoon tahini
- 1 teaspoon salt
- ¼ teaspoon chilli/chili powder
- 2 garlic cloves
- 1 tablespoon sweet paprika
- 1 red (bell) pepper, seeded
- umeboshi vinegar, to taste (or substitute with lemon juice and a little soy sauce)
- 2–3 slices of rustic bread
- garlic chives and mixed micro cress or herbs, to garnish

SERVES 2-3

Cover the walnuts with plenty of water and let soak for a couple of hours or overnight with a pinch of salt. Rinse and drain, then place in a high-speed blender with all the remaining ingredients (except the bread and the garnish) and blend for 1 minute into a velvety hummus. For weaker blenders, you might need to add a little water during blending.

Toast the bread and slice into bite-sized pieces. Top each piece of a spoonful of the pâté and garnish with the herbs or micro cress, then arrange on a serving platter. Any leftover pâté can be served as a dip.

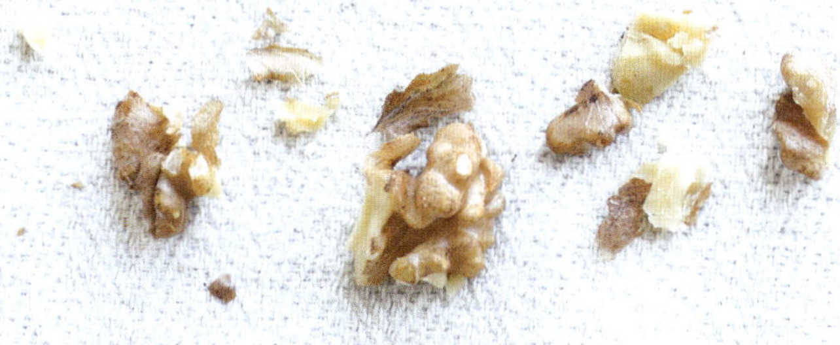

BABY WELSH 'RARE-BITES'

These bite-sized pieces of ciabatta are so perfect for sharing. Topped with a luxurious béchamel sauce, they are very moreish.

1 ciabatta roll
vegetable oil

BÉCHAMEL SAUCE
40 g/3 tablespoons butter
25 g/3 tablespoons plain/all-purpose flour
100 ml/$^1/_3$ cup milk
300 ml/1$^1/_4$ cups ale
Worcestershire sauce
1 teaspoon English mustard
150 g/2 cups grated/shredded Parmesan cheese
150 g/1$^2/_3$ cups grated/shredded Cheddar cheese
salt, to taste

TOPPING
50 g/generous $^1/_2$ cup grated/shredded Parmesan cheese
50 g/$^1/_2$ cup grated/shredded Cheddar cheese

MAKES ABOUT 12

For the béchamel sauce, in a small saucepan, heat the butter and flour over a medium heat. Leave on the heat until the butter is foaming, then whisk the mixture to a smooth paste. With the pan still on the heat, add all the milk and whisk until thoroughly combined. Slowly, add the ale, whisking to make a light brown sauce with a cream-like consistency.

Add a couple of glugs of Worcestershire sauce and the mustard before adding the grated/shredded cheeses. Whisk over a low heat until a cheesy, ale-infused, béchamel sauce is formed. Add a generous pinch of salt to taste. Add a little more Worcestershire sauce and mustard if you prefer a stronger flavour.

Your sauce is now made. It is easier to use when chilled, so make it in advance if you can and refrigerate (the sauce will keep for several days in the fridge). The recipe makes more than you need for one batch of Welsh Rarebit so you can freeze what you won't use this time.

Preheat the oven to 140°C fan/160°C/325°F/Gas 3.

For the toast, thinly slice a ciabatta roll and drizzle with a little oil. Place on a baking sheet and bake in the preheated oven for 5 minutes, until browned and crispy.

To finish, spread a generous portion of the béchamel sauce on each piece of toast, then add a sprinkle of the mixed topping cheeses. Bake in the preheated oven for 5–7 minutes until golden brown on top.

CHERRY TOMATO BRUSCHETTA

Juicy tomatoes contrast nicely with the crunchiness of the baked bread in this vibrant, classic Italian snack. Serve as a rustic start to a meal, a midday snack or lunchtime treat. **See photo on page 104.**

1 slender baguette
2 teaspoons olive oil
12 red and yellow cherry tomatoes, quartered
1 teaspoon balsamic vinegar
a pinch of salt
1 garlic clove, peeled
4–6 fresh basil leaves, plus extra to garnish
freshly ground black pepper

MAKES ABOUT 12

Preheat the oven to 180°C fan/200°C/400°F/Gas 6.

Slice the baguette into 1-cm/½-inch thick slices. Transfer to a baking sheet and lightly brush with 1 teaspoon of the olive oil. Bake in the preheated oven for 20 minutes, until pale gold and crisp. Remove from the oven and set aside to cool.

Meanwhile, mix together the cherry tomato quarters with the remaining olive oil, balsamic vinegar, salt and whole garlic clove in a large bowl. Shred the basil leaves and mix in. Set aside to allow the flavours to infuse while the baguette slices bake and cool.

Discard the garlic clove from the tomato mixture, then spoon onto each slice of bread. Garnish with basil leaves and sprinkle with pepper. Serve at once.

PORCINI & WILD MUSHROOM CROSTINI

Combining three different types of mushroom (porcini, chestnut and chanterelle) in a creamy sauce with a hint of truffle, this crostini topping is simply sublime. **See photo on page 105.**

- 40 crostini (see page 118)
- 30 g/1 oz. dried porcini mushrooms
- 200 g/7 oz. baby chestnut mushrooms
- 100 g/3½ oz. chanterelle mushrooms
- ½ tablespoon unsalted butter
- ½ tablespoon olive oil
- 5 teaspoons truffle porcini paste
- 150 ml/generous ½ cup double/heavy cream
- 1 tablespoon freshly snipped chives
- salt and freshly ground black pepper

MAKES 40

First, make the crostini (see page 118). This step can be done a week before and the crostini kept in an airtight container.

Soak the porcini mushrooms in boiling water for at least 20 minutes. Meanwhile, slice the fresh mushrooms, and then slice the soaked porcini.

Heat the butter and olive oil in a frying pan/skillet over a fairly high heat. Add the mushrooms and fry for 10 minutes, then add the truffled porcini paste and the cream. Reduce the cream a little, then season to taste.

Spread a teaspoon on each crostini and top with some chives. Serve.

TRUFFLED CANAPÉ TOASTS

Two different truffle-flavoured toppings make these crostini perfect to serve with a pre-dinner drink.

1 baguette, cut into 16 slices, 5-mm/¼-inch thick
1 tablespoon olive oil

TRUFFLED MUSHROOM PASTE
10 g/⅓ oz. dried porcini
1 tablespoon olive oil
½ shallot, finely chopped
120 g/4 oz. white/cup mushrooms, chopped
1 teaspoon brandy
½ teaspoon truffle oil
1 tablespoon mascarpone cheese
salt and freshly ground black pepper
½ tablespoon pine nuts, toasted, to garnish
freshly chopped flat-leaf parsley, to garnish

TRUFFLE HONEY MUSHROOMS
80 g/3 oz. soft goat's cheese
1 tablespoon truffle honey
1 white/cup mushroom, cut into 8 thin slices
freshly ground black pepper

MAKES 16

Preheat the oven to 160°C fan/180°C/350°F/Gas 4.

Place the baguette slices on a baking sheet, brush lightly with the olive oil and bake in the preheated oven for 15 minutes until browned. Set aside to cool.

For the paste topping, pour boiling water over the dried porcini; set aside for 20 minutes, then strain. Heat the olive oil in a frying pan/skillet. Add the shallot and fry gently until softened, then add the soaked porcini, mushrooms and brandy and cook over a medium heat, stirring, for 1–2 minutes. Season, then fry, stirring, until the mushrooms have softened. Set aside to cool.

In a food processor blend together the cooled mushroom mixture, truffle oil and mascarpone cheese to a smooth paste. Spread half the baguette slices with the truffled mushroom paste. Garnish with pine nuts and parsley.

Spread the remaining baguette slices with goat's cheese. Drizzle each one with a little of the truffle honey and top with a mushroom slice. Season with black pepper.

BROAD BEAN, RICOTTA & FETA CROSTINI
with pancetta

- 10 slices/strips pancetta
- 300 g/2¼ cups frozen petits pois
- 200 g/1¼ cups broad/fava beans, fresh or frozen
- 1 tablespoon olive oil
- grated zest of ½ lemon
- 100 g/3½ oz. ricotta
- 10 freshly chopped mint leaves, plus 10 leaves, to garnish
- salt and freshly ground black pepper
- 40 crostini (see page 118)
- 200 g/7 oz. feta, crumbled

MAKES 40

Preheat the oven to 160°C fan/180°C/350°F/ Gas 4.

Cut each slice/strip of pancetta crossways into 4. Put the pancetta onto a baking sheet and bake in the preheated oven for 10 minutes, or until crisp. Drain any excess fat on paper towels and set aside.

Put the frozen petits pois in a pan of boiling water for 1 minute, then plunge into cold water. Repeat with the beans and then squeeze them out of their skins.

Put the petits pois and half of the beans into a food processor or blender. Blend together with the olive oil, lemon zest, ricotta, mint, salt and pepper.

Spread a teaspoonful of the mix on top of each crostini, followed by a little feta, chopped mint, remaining beans and piece of pancetta. Serve.

MEDITERRANEAN VEGETABLE CROSTINI
with pesto

- 4 tablespoons olive oil
- 1 red (bell) pepper
- ½ aubergine/eggplant, thinly sliced
- 1 courgette/zucchini, thinly sliced
- ¼ red onion, cut into wedges (optional)
- 1 x 125-g/4½-oz. mozzarella ball
- 40 crostini (see page 118)

PESTO

- 50 g/generous ⅓ cup pine nuts
- 40 g/1½ oz. fresh basil leaves
- 1 garlic clove
- 60 g/1 cup freshly grated/shredded Parmesan cheese
- 3 tablespoons olive oil
- a squeeze of fresh lemon juice
- freshly ground black pepper

MAKES 40

Preheat the oven to 180°C fan/200°C/400°F/ Gas 6.

For the pesto, place the pine nuts in a dry frying pan/skillet and toast lightly over low-medium heat for a few minutes, shaking the pan often. Let cool, then put in a food processor or blender with the other ingredients and blitz until smooth.

Rub a little oil onto the red (bell) pepper and roast in the oven until the skin blisters and turns black. Remove from oven, wrap in foil and, when cool enough, remove the skin. Slice into thin strips. Brush the aubergine/eggplant, courgette/zucchini and red onion, if using, with olive oil and chargrill/broil on high for 2–3 minutes on each side.

Divide the mozzarella ball into quarters. Then divide each quarter into 10 pieces. Spread ½ teaspoon of pesto on each crostini and top with the mozzarella and vegetables. Season with a little pepper and serve.

PEA & MINT CROSTINI

Peas and mint make such a heavenly combination, especially on top of a crunchy crostini. You can use frozen peas if fresh ones are not in season.

10–12 slices of baguette
60 ml/4 tablespoons extra virgin olive oil
1 garlic clove, cut in half
250 g/1 2/3 cups fresh peas (or 250 g/2 cups frozen peas)
a small handful of young fresh mint leaves, roughly chopped, plus extra to garnish
salt, to season
zest of 1 lemon, to garnish

MAKES 10-12

Preheat the oven to 160°C fan/180°C/350°F/ Gas 4.

Brush the baguette slices with a little of the oil and place on a baking sheet. Cook in the preheated oven for about 10 minutes until golden and crisp. Remove from the oven and rub lightly with the cut side of the garlic clove.

If using fresh peas, cook them in boiling salted water for about 3 minutes, drain and pop into a blender. If using frozen, simply defrost and put straight into the blender. Add the remaining oil and whizz to a lightly textured purée. Remove from the blender and stir in the mint.

Form the pea mixture into neat quenelles using two teaspoons and top the crostini. Scatter with a little lemon zest and a few extra mint leaves and serve.

SALT COD CROSTINI

Laced with garlic and speckled with herbs, this salt cod topping is a delight. Note that you need to soak the fish for 48 hours before blending, changing the water often.

500 g/1 lb. 2 oz. salt cod, soaked for 48 hours
570 ml/2 1/4 cups whole milk
2 fresh bay leaves
1 tablespoon black peppercorns
2 garlic cloves
120 ml/1/2 cup extra virgin olive oil, plus extra for brushing
a handful of fresh flat-leaf parsley, finely chopped
12 slices of baguette, baked as left
salt and black pepper, to season

MAKES 12

Preheat the oven to 160°C fan/180°C/350°F/ Gas 4.

Place the pre-soaked cod in a large saucepan and pour in the milk. Add the bay leaves, peppercorns, garlic and enough water to cover the fish. Set over a medium heat and simmer for 20 minutes or so, until just cooked. Remove the fish from the milk and strain out the bits and bobs, reserving the milk and the garlic.

Meanwhile, when the fish has cooled a little, flake it carefully into the bowl of a food processor or blender, taking care to remove the bones. Add half of the olive oil, a little of the reserved milk and the softened garlic and pulse, adding the remaining oil and as much milk as necessary, until the mixture has a similar thickness to that of creamy mashed potato. Stir in the parsley, adjust the seasoning and use it to top the crostini.

GORGONZOLA & ANCHOVY CROSTINI with pickled radicchio

The sweet and sour flavours of this quick pickled radicchio/Italian chicory perfectly offset the Gorgonzola cheese and anchovies, and the colour contrast makes for the prettiest of canapés.

12 slices of baguette
3–4 tablespoons extra virgin olive oil
300 g/2½ cups Gorgonzola
12 canned anchovies

PICKLED RADICCHIO
300 ml/1¼ cups apple vinegar
1 generous tablespoon runny honey
1 teaspoon fennel seeds
1 small long radicchio/Italian chicory, sliced

MAKES 12

To pickle the radicchio/Italian chicory, pour the apple vinegar into a large saucepan and bring to the boil. Boil for a couple of minutes, then add the honey and fennel seeds. Turn the heat down and bubble for 5 minutes. Drop the sliced radicchio/Italian chicory into the vinegar, cook for 1 minute, then turn off the heat. After 4–5 minutes, remove the radicchio/Italian chicory and fennel seeds with a slotted spoon, transfer to a mixing bowl and cool.

Brush the baguette slices with the oil and toast on a hot griddle/ridged stovetop pan until golden (alternatively bake in an oven preheated to 160°C fan/180°C/350°F/Gas 4 for 10 minutes or so).

Top each crostini with a good dollop of Gorgonzola cheese and add a single anchovy. Garnish with the pickled radicchio/Italian chicory and serve.

SWEET TOAST

SWEET TOAST TRIO

Treat yourself to these delicious toppings, combining nut butters, seeds, fresh fruit and a homemade chocolate spread.

PEANUT BUTTER & BERRY

Like PB & J, only way better...

2 slices of bread
2 tablespoons peanut butter
50–60 g/$^1/_3$–$^1/_2$ cup fresh berries
  or thawed frozen berries
honey, to serve
hemp seeds, to serve

SERVES 1

Toast the bread to your desired toastiness. Slather on peanut butter. Top with berries, a drizzle of honey and a sprinkle of hemp seeds.

BANANA & SEED

Natural sweetness with a little crunch.

2 slices of bread
2 tablespoons almond butter
1 banana, sliced into rounds
$^1/_2$ teaspoon hemp seeds
$^1/_2$ teaspoon chia seeds
1 teaspoon pumpkin seeds/pepitas

SERVES 1

Toast the bread to your desired toastiness. Spread with a generous amount of almond butter. Top with banana slices and sprinkle on the seeds.

HAZELNUT CHOC SPREAD

This recipe makes more chocolate spread than needed for 1 serving, but it keeps well in the fridge for 2 weeks.

130 g/1 cup blanched hazelnuts
2 tablespoons melted coconut oil
2 tablespoons maple syrup or honey
2 tablespoons cocoa powder
1 teaspoon vanilla extract
a pinch of sea salt
2 slices of bread
sliced strawberries, to serve
toasted hazelnuts, roughly chopped,
  to serve (optional)

SERVES 1

Preheat the oven to 160°C fan/180°C/350°F/ Gas 4.

Spread the hazelnuts out on a dry baking sheet. Pop in the preheated oven for 5 minutes, shake the sheet and return to the oven for another 5 minutes until lightly toasted.

Transfer to a food processor or high speed blender and process for about 5–8 minutes. Push beyond the fine powder until you get a denser, softened nut butter.

Add the melted coconut oil, syrup or honey, cocoa powder, vanilla extract and sea salt and blend for 1–2 minutes until fairly smooth.

Toast the bread, then spread with the chocolate spread and top with sliced strawberries and chopped toasted hazelnuts, if liked.

FRESH FIGS & TAHINI ON TOAST
with pistachios & honey

Nutty, sweet and just the tiniest bit salty, this is one of the most glorious ways to enjoy figs when they're in season. Sprinkle with a few chopped pistachios for the perfect finishing touch.

2 slices of bread
2–3 tablespoons tahini
3–4 fresh figs, sliced

TO SERVE
runny honey
a pinch of flaky sea salt, such as Maldon
chopped pistachios

SERVES 1

Toast the bread to your liking. Smear with tahini and top with sliced figs. Drizzle with honey and sprinkle with sea salt and chopped pistachios to serve.

CINNAMON FRENCH TOAST

Cinnamon is used in abundance in these indulgent French toasts as the bread is sandwiched together with a sweet cinnamon butter and the egg batter also contains ground cinnamon. Serve with fresh berries if you wish.

8 slices of white bread, crusts removed
4 eggs
60 ml/$^{1}/_{4}$ cup milk
2 teaspoons ground cinnamon
1 tablespoon caster/granulated sugar
1–2 tablespoons butter, for frying
sugar nibs/pearl sugar or caster/granulated sugar, for sprinkling
icing/confectioners' sugar, to dust

FILLING
100 g/7 tablespoons butter, softened
1 teaspoon vanilla sugar
50 g/$^{1}/_{4}$ cup caster/granulated sugar
2 teaspoons ground cinnamon

SERVES 4

For the filling, mix together the butter, vanilla sugar, caster/granulated sugar and cinnamon to a smooth paste using a spoon or a fork.

Spread a thick layer of filling over 4 of the slices of bread and place a second slice of bread on top of each to sandwich the butter in the middle. Press the sandwiches down so that the filling will not leak.

For the French toast, whisk together the eggs, milk, cinnamon and sugar in a mixing bowl, transfer to a shallow dish and set aside. Melt the butter in a large frying pan/skillet set over a medium heat until the butter begins to foam. Soak each sandwich in the egg mixture on one side for a few seconds, then turn over and soak the other side. The bread should be fully coated in egg, but not too soggy – it is best to soak one sandwich at a time.

Put each sandwich straight into the frying pan/skillet with the melted butter set over a medium heat before soaking the next sandwich. Sprinkle the tops of the sandwiches with a little pearl sugar and cook for 2–3 minutes. Once the sandwiches are golden brown underneath, turn over and cook for a few minutes longer. The pearl sugar will caramelize and create a lightly crusty topping. Keep the cooked toast warm while you cook the remaining slices in the same way, adding a little butter to the pan each time, if required.

Serve immediately, sliced and dusted with icing/confectioners' sugar.

LABNA, ROASTED GRAPE & WALNUT TARTINES

Labna is a strained yogurt cheese - it's easy to make, but you need patience while it drains. Here it is spread on toasted sourdough bread and topped with blistered red grapes and walnuts.

60 red grapes (a medium bunch)
100 g/¾ cup (about 40) walnuts, roughly chopped
2 tablespoons olive oil
1 teaspoon sugar
4 slices of sourdough bread
½ garlic clove
salt and freshly ground black pepper

LABNA
250 g/1 cup full-fat Greek yogurt
1 teaspoon salt

SERVES 4

Begin the labna at least 6 hours before you plan on eating. Mix together the Greek yogurt and the salt. Line a sieve/strainer with 2 pieces of muslin/cheesecloth. Set the sieve and the cloth over a bowl. Pour the yogurt and the salt into the strainer, cover the top with the ends of the cloth and allow to strain for at least 6 hours.

After 6 hours, squeeze the cloth to help the curds separate from the whey. The yogurt should have the consistency of cream cheese. You should end up with 125 g/½ cup labna. Transfer to a covered container and chill in the fridge until ready to use. Alternatively, you can roll it into small balls and cover them with olive oil (it will last in the fridge for about 1 week).

Preheat the oven to 200°C fan/220°C/425°F/Gas 7. Put the grapes and walnuts on a baking sheet. Sprinkle with olive oil and sugar. Roast for 20 minutes, until the grapes have started to wrinkle. Toast the sourdough. When it is nicely brown, rub the toast with the cut side of the garlic.

Spread the slices of toasted sourdough with a tablespoon of labna, then pile on the grapes and walnuts. Season generously with salt and pepper.

BANANA CHOC CHIP FRENCH TOAST

The combination of warm banana and melted chocolate with a crunchy toasty crust makes for a fantastic dessert - or a treat at any time of the day!

1 ripe banana, peeled and sliced
freshly squeezed juice of ½ a lemon
50 g/⅓ cup milk/semi-sweet chocolate chips
100 g/1⅓ cups dried banana chips
4 thick slices of brioche or white bread
2 eggs
80 ml/scant ⅓ cup double/heavy cream
1 tablespoon caster/granulated sugar
1 teaspoon ground cinnamon
1–2 tablespoons butter, for frying
icing/confectioners' sugar, to dust

SERVES 4

Begin by preparing the filling. In a mixing bowl, use a fork to mash the banana with the lemon juice to a smooth purée. Stir in the chocolate chips and set aside.

Blitz the banana chips to fine crumbs in a food processor. Tip onto a plate and set aside.

Using a sharp knife, cut a pocket in the top of each brioche slice to create a large cavity. Take care not to cut all the way through as it is this cavity which will hold your filling. Spoon some of the filling into each slice and press the opening down to close the pocket.

Whisk together the eggs, cream, caster/granulated sugar and cinnamon in a mixing bowl, transfer to a shallow dish and set aside. Melt the butter in a large frying pan/skillet set over a medium heat until the butter begins to foam. Soak each filled slice in the egg mixture on one side for a few seconds, then turn over and soak the other side. The slices should be fully coated in egg, but not too soggy – it is best to soak one slice at a time. Carefully move bread to the banana chip plate and coat in fine crumbs on both sides. Put each slice straight in the pan before soaking and cooking the next slice.

Cook for a few minutes on each side until the bread is golden brown, but taking care that the banana chips do not burn. Keep the cooked toast warm while you cook the remaining slices in the same way, adding a little butter to the pan each time, if required.

Cut the slices into quarters, then dust with icing/confectioners' sugar and serve.

CRUNCHY PECAN PIE FRENCH TOAST

This is inspired by the classic pecan pie, with a crunchy nut coating and an indulgent buttery toffee sauce to pour over.

2 eggs
80 ml/scant 1/3 cup double/heavy cream
1 teaspoon ground cinnamon
1 tablespoon caster/granulated sugar
1 teaspoon vanilla extract/vanilla bean paste
140 g/3/4 cup pecan nuts, finely chopped
1–2 tablespoons butter, for frying
4 slices of white bread

TOFFEE SAUCE

40 g/scant 1/4 cup caster/granulated sugar
40 g/scant 1/4 cup muscovado sugar
1 teaspoon ground cinnamon
1 teaspoon vanilla extract/vanilla bean paste
2 tablespoons butter
2 tablespoons golden syrup/light corn syrup
60 ml/1/4 cup double/heavy cream

SERVES 4

Begin by preparing the toffee sauce. Put the caster/granulated and muscovado sugars, cinnamon, vanilla extract/vanilla bean paste, butter and golden syrup/light corn syrup in a saucepan or pot set over a medium heat. Simmer until the sugar has dissolved, then add the cream and whisk. Heat for a few minutes longer. Keep the pan on the heat but turn it down to low to keep the sauce warm until you are ready to serve.

For the French toast, whisk together the eggs, cream, cinnamon, sugar and vanilla extract/vanilla bean paste until the mixture is smooth. Place the egg mixture in a wide, shallow dish and the chopped pecans on a plate. Melt the butter in a large frying pan/skillet set over a medium heat until the butter begins to foam. Soak each slice in the egg mixture on one side for a few seconds, then turn over and soak the other side. The slices should be fully coated in egg, but not too soggy – it is best to soak one slice at a time. Carefully move the bread to the pecan plate and coat in pecan crumbs on both sides. Put each slice straight in the pan before soaking and cooking the next slice.

Cook for a few minutes on each side until the slices are golden brown, but taking care that the nuts do not burn. Keep the cooked toast warm while you cook the remaining slices in the same way, adding a little butter to the pan each time, if required.

Serve the toasts with the warm sauce.

HONEY ROAST FIGS & ORANGE MASCARPONE FRENCH TOAST

with toasted almonds

In this citrus version of French toast, the orange mascarpone topping perfectly cuts through the thick, eggy brioche for a delicious treat.

125 ml/1/2 cup mascarpone
2 tablespoons single/light cream
1/2 teaspoon grated orange zest, plus extra to serve
1 tablespoon freshly squeezed orange juice
4 ripe figs, cut in half lengthways
clear honey, to drizzle
100 g/3 1/2 oz. whole almonds
2 eggs
100 ml/1/3 cup milk
1/4 teaspoon pure vanilla extract
1 tablespoon caster/granulated sugar
2–4 thick slices of brioche
unsalted butter, for frying
icing/confectioners' sugar, for dusting

2 baking sheets, greased and lined with baking parchment

SERVES 2

Preheat the oven to 160°C fan/180°C/350°F/Gas 4.

Mix the mascarpone with the cream, orange zest and juice in a small mixing bowl. Cover and set aside.

Place the figs, cut-side up, on the prepared baking sheet. Drizzle with honey and roast in the preheated oven for 15–20 minutes until soft and caramelized. Remove from the oven and set aside. Scatter the almonds on the other prepared baking sheet and bake in the oven for 8–10 minutes until lightly golden. Remove from the oven, cool completely, then roughly chop if desired.

To make the French toast, whisk together the eggs with the milk in a large mixing bowl. Add the vanilla and caster/granulated sugar, and whisk again. Transfer to a shallow dish and set aside.

Melt a little butter in a large frying pan/skillet set over a medium heat. Dip each slice of brioche in the egg mixture one at a time. Let the slices soak up the mixture for a few seconds, then turn over to coat the other side.

Place the egg-soaked brioche in the hot pan, one slice at a time, and cook until golden on the bottom. Turn over and cook for a few minutes longer until both sides are golden. Transfer to a clean baking sheet and put in the oven to keep warm. Cook the remaining slices in the same way, adding a little more butter to the pan, if required.

To serve, cut the brioche slices in half, overlap the slices on the plate and top with the figs, mascarpone and almonds. Sprinkle with a little orange zest and icing/confectioners' sugar.

PEANUT BUTTER & JELLY FRENCH TOAST

Peanut butter and jelly is a classic American combination. These French toasts are coated in sweet honey-roasted peanuts, but if you like salty flavours you could replace them with crushed salted peanuts instead.

- 4 large thick slices of brioche or white bread
- 120 g/1 cup honey roasted peanuts
- 4 eggs
- 120 ml/scant 1/2 cup double/heavy cream
- 1 tablespoon caster/granulated sugar
- a pinch of salt
- 1–2 tablespoons butter, for greasing
- icing/confectioners' sugar, for dusting

FILLING

- 3 tablespoons crunchy peanut butter
- 3 tablespoons fruit jam/jelly (flavour of your choosing)

SERVES 4

Using a sharp knife, cut a pocket in the top of each brioche slice to create a large cavity. Take care not to cut all the way through as it is this cavity which will hold your filling. Carefully spread some peanut butter and jam/jelly inside each pocket using a knife, then press the opening down to close the pocket.

Put the peanuts in a food processor and pulse to a fine crumb, then tip onto a large plate and set aside.

Whisk together the eggs, cream, caster/granulated sugar and salt in a mixing bowl, transfer to a shallow dish and set aside. Melt the butter in a large frying pan/skillet set over a medium heat until the butter begins to foam. Soak each filled slice in the egg mixture on one side for a few seconds, then turn over and soak the other side. The slices should be fully coated in egg, but not too soggy – it is best to soak one slice at a time. Carefully move the slices to the peanut plate and coat in fine crumbs on both sides. Put each slice straight in the pan before soaking and cooking the next slice.

Cook for a few minutes on each side until the slices are golden brown, but take care that the nuts do not burn. Keep the cooked toast warm while you cook the remaining slices in the same way, adding a little butter to the pan each time, if required.

Serve the toasts immediately, dusted with icing/confectioners' sugar.

VANILLA FRENCH TOAST with red berries

These toasts are the perfect treat when berries are in season. Raspberries, blackberries, blueberries, strawberries - just pick your favourite and pile them high on the vanilla toasts.

2 UK large/US extra large eggs
a splash of milk
1 teaspoon vanilla extract
1 teaspoon olive oil
4 thick slices of white bread
1 lemon, cut into wedges
fresh berries and icing/
confectioners' sugar,
to serve

SERVES 4

Crack the eggs into a wide bowl, add the milk and vanilla extract and whisk it all together.

Heat the oil in a frying pan/skillet over a medium-high heat. Dip the bread slices in the egg mixture and place them in the pan. Cook, turning the pieces over so they are golden brown on both sides.

Serve with a squeeze of lemon, a pile of fresh berries and a dusting of icing/confectioners' sugar.

INDEX

RECIPE CREDITS

Laura Washburn Hutton
Avocado & refried bean toastie with tomatillo salsa
Avocado, tomato, spinach & smoked chicken toastie
Basic grilled cheese sandwich
BBQ ham hock & mac 'n' cheese pan-fried toastie
Brie & apple-cranberry sauce walnut bread toastie
Cheddar toastie with quick homemade red onion chutney
Chicory, blue cheese, Serrano & walnut pesto pan-fried toastie
Chorizo, mini peppers & Manchego toastie
Leek & Gruyère toastie with Dijon mustard
Lobster & Beaufort brioche toastie with tarragon mayo
Kimchi & Cheddar toastie
Pickled beetroot & goat's cheese brioche toastie

Mat Follas
Baby Welsh 'rare-bites'
Broad bean hummus
Chicken liver pâté on toast
Rarebits with shaved truffle
Salt cod brandade with toasted baguette slices
Spiced crab on ciabatta toast
Summer sardines on toast
Trout pâté with melba toasts

Jenny Linford
Buttery eggs with chanterelles
Cherry tomato bruschetta
Fettunta
Pan Catalan
Supper mushrooms two ways
Truffled canapé toasts

Hannah Miles
Banana choc chip French toast
Cinnamon French toast
Crunchy pecan pie French toast
Curry spice French toast with coconut chutney
Italian tricolore toastie
Peanut butter & jelly French toast

Shelagh Ryan
Apple & ginger jam
Cheese on toast with kasoundi
Honey roast figs & orange mascarpone French toast
Hot steak sandwich with beetroot jam & blue cheese dressing
Sautéed mushrooms & lemon herbed feta on sourdough toast
Smashed avocado with courgette ribbons & dukkah

Dunja Gulin
Baked kidney bean falafel
Creamy cashew & avocado toasts with garlic chives
Tofu & brown rice hummus with red cabbage & pea shoots
Tofu, mushroom & asparagus scramble with turmeric
Walnut & red pepper pâté on mini toasts

Leah Vanderveldt
Fresh figs & tahini on toast with pistachios & honey
Garlicky peas & spinach with goat's cheese
Roasted carrot & hummus
Smashed avocado on sourdough
Sweet toast trio

Tori Haschka
Labna, roasted grape & walnut tartines
Mushrooms, brown butter & Parmesan on sourdough toast
Ricotta, mint, chilli & lemon with griddle sourdough toasts
Steak tartare with mustard cheese toasts

Carol Hilker
Fisherman's Wharf benedict on sourdough
Fried eggs in a hole
Grape jelly
Lemon curd

Liz Franklin
Gorgonzola & anchovy crostini with pickled radicchio
Pea & mint crostini
Salt cod crostini

Tonia George
Baked beans with maple syrup & paprika
Poached eggs & spinach on toasted flatbread
Scrambled eggs, smoked trout & shiso on toast

Milli Taylor
Broad bean, ricotta & feta crostini with pancetta
Mediterranean vegetable crostini with pesto
Porcini & wild mushroom crostini

Miranda Ballard
Cured duck & Dijon mustard on garlic bruschetta
Serrano ham & aubergine on toasted soda bread

Jordan & Jessica Bourke
New-York style avocado & tomatoes on rye toast
Scrambled eggs on spelt toast

Laura Santini
Ultimate tuna melt toast

Janet Sawyer
Vanilla French toast with red berries

PHOTOGRAPHY CREDITS

Tim Atkins Page 70

Peter Cassidy Page 104

Helen Cathcart Pages 105, 116

Jonathan Gregson Pages 12, 23, 33, 45

Mowie Kay Pages 59, 60, 108, 119, 120

Adrian Lawrence Pages 3, 55

Steve Painter Pages 2, 32, 39, 43, 46, 49, 50, 53, 54, 56, 63, 76, 78, 79, 81, 82, 85, 89, 93, 94, 98, 101, 102, 111, 123, 129, 133, 134, 138, 141

Con Poulos Page 40

William Reavell Pages 6, 69, 76

Toby Scott Pages 19, 24, 28

Kate Whitaker Pages 8, 9, 27, 31, 36, 97, 122, 137

Isobel Wield Pages 11, 73, 90, 130

Clare Winfield Pages 1, 16, 35, 64, 107, 115, 125, 126